6-23
HHR

D1087924

testimony of the invisible man

WILLIAM CARLOS WILLIAMS

FRANCIS PONGE

RAINER MARIA RILKE

PABLO NERUDA

BY NANCY WILLARD

UNIVERSITY OF MISSOURI PRESS
COLUMBIA, MISSOURI

testimony of the invisible man

520006

In addition, I wish to acknowledge the permissions courteously granted by the editors of the following magazines, in which my articles first appeared:

Chelsea 22/23 for assignment of my article, "Radiant Bread for the Sun of Man," originally published in the issue for June, 1968;

Comparative Literature, for permission to reprint "A Poetry of Things," which appeared first in the issue for Fall, 1965;

Shenandoah: The Washington and Lee University Review for my article, "Testimony of the Invisible Man," which was first published in the issue for Autumn, 1967.

For my mother and father
and Morris Greenhut

preface

Nancy Willard has chosen for her study of four poets three of the very ones I myself care most about among the writers who came to maturity in the early twentieth century: Williams, Rilke, Ponge. Her fourth choice, Neruda, has thus far not gripped me in the same way, though I have long had the feeling his work would be an experience I would come to some day, at the right time.

For a year, at Vassar College, I worked alongside Nancy Willard. We discussed our students — some of mine had been hers the year before — and the war, and the peace movement; and surely we from time to time talked about poetry other than that which our students were writing: Yes, I remember in particular our showing one another poems by Robert Duncan and Thomas Merton. Yet, though I was little by little coming to know her own fine and developing work in poetry, I had no idea she shared so closely my own preoccupations, my own masters. How isolated we can be, even amongst friends! So it was with a curious shock of pleasure that I heard about this book.

Because of my inadequate knowledge of German, Rilke's influence, for me, has been more profoundly through the Letters (especially those translated by R. F. C. Hull and published by Macmillan in England) than the poems. Read over and over, from 1946 on, passages in these letters, referring to an attitude to the material world — an attitude of reverent attention — through which it was possible for a poet to attain to song, have been paramount formative factors in my life. Only Williams, of all the masters, has been equally important for me.

When I came to Williams I was already partly formed by Rilke; and where Rilke had given insight into what it was, essentially, to be a poet, Williams opened up the language in which to live those insights and made it clear to me (more clear than, reading Rilke in translation or, if in German, only with much help from a facing version, I had realized before 1950 — though from then on it became a constant concern) that for the poet there was no vision without language, no reality without language, that the sound and rhythm of the poem *are* the poem, thing among things.

There was a time — years ago — when I felt puzzled by what then seemed contradictory in all that these two great poets seemed to represent. It is easy to find superficial polarities: to see Rilke as aristocratic, mystical, and concerned with "high language," Williams as democratic, pragmatic, and devoted to contemporary idiom, for instance. I did not try to worry the matter through to a conclusion. It seemed enough to care so much about them both and to know the ferment of them both working in my life. Now Nancy Willard, without troubling her head about polarities, calmly — and just at a time when Rilke's poems are coming to me with fresh reality through the (mainly still-unpublished) versions of a young American poet, George Quasha — places both upon a common ground, that same ground of open, devoted, curious, loving attention to *things* where Ponge so emphatically stands also. It is always a betrayal to effect reconciliations merely by ignoring distinctions; but to point out what *is* shared by two such different poets is not a betrayal but an act not unrelated to what Rilke said love was, "a mutual bordering and guarding of two solitudes."

Ponge is a poet I came to much later than to Rilke and Williams and whose work I don't pretend to yet know well, but who began to become important for me from the moment I first read the lines about an oyster that are cited in Chapter III of this book. The icy spring water of Ponge's phenomenological clarity — I am thinking here of Gaston Bachelard's use of the term — is both familiar and enticing to one who has taken "No ideas but in things" seriously, not mistaking it for "No ideas," but understanding that it means the poet can discover the universal only in the local — in the concrete particulars both of the material world and of language itself. Ponge's intelligence is a precision tool and in constant use; he is full of ideas; but they are embodied, incarnate, in *the thing observed.* Or rather, the things observed do not illustrate the ideas, but give rise to them. Like Williams (and of course, one may say like all good poets) he exemplifies the fact that the poet's task is to discover, not to prove.

Though I have thought I detected in some Neruda poems a rhetoric I distrusted, that is, an overextension of feeling and language, one has only to read some of the poems quoted in Chapter IV — for example, the "Oda al Elefante" — to note that here too, song arises from precise and open vision.

It is a virtue of these essays that parallels are not forced. Nancy Willard does not try to squeeze all four poets into one small esthetic rowboat. But I think she does a service in juxtaposing for us what is genuinely related in their concern and thus making understandable how it happens that they can live side by side as powerful forces, yet not in conflict, in the minds of other writers. If I find myself wishing she had focused not only on the correspondences in their basic attitudes but on their very different senses of form and rhythm, I qualify that wish by the recognition that this book, by its very nature — as a first map of an intuited territory, a place in imagination where Nancy Willard wants, as I do, to find her own bearings and live — is a beginning, not an end.

Denise Levertov

July, 1968

acknowledgments

I am pleased to acknowledge the material assistance given me in the production of this work by Vassar College, through a generous allowance from the Salmon Fund. To the Department of English of the College I am grateful for a grant that helped me to complete the manuscript, and to Norma Feldkamp who typed the manuscript, and to Susan Allard who proofread it and constructed the Index.

My translations of Francis Ponge's "The Sun of the Abyss" were assisted by my reading of Lane Dunlop's version, which appeared in *Harper's Bazaar* for January, 1967. A book of Ponge's work in translation is being edited by Mr. Dunlop for Jonathan Cape, Ltd. Mrs. William Carlos Williams graciously granted permission to quote "Tribute to Neruda, the poet collector of seashells," which appears as epigraph to this work. The poem appeared in the *Rutgers Review* for Spring, 1967.

I am happy to acknowledge my indebtedness to the following publishers, who permitted use of materials on which they hold copyright: Astor-Honor, Inc., Beacon Press, *Chelsea, Comparative Literature*, Editorial Losada S.A., Editions Gallimard, Grove Press, Inc., The Hogarth Press, Inc., Insel Verlag, *Mainstream*, Max Niehans Verlag, Methuen & Co., Ltd., New Directions Publishing Corporation, W. W. Norton & Company, Inc., *Poetry*, Penguin Books, Ltd., Philosophical Library, Random House, Inc., and *Shenandoah*: The Washington and Lee University Review. Señor Pablo Neruda allowed me to quote extensively from his work, and Mr. Victor Perera permitted use of his translation of Neruda's "Walking Around." I trust that my use of these works will attract more readers to the other creations of the four poets I have discussed.

N.W.

Poughkeepsie, New York
September, 1969

contents

1. A Poetry of Things,   1

2. A Local Habitation: William Carlos Williams,   16

3. The Common Life With a Star: Francis Ponge,   43

4. How to Live: Rainer Maria Rilke,   61

5. Radiant Bread for the Sun of Man: Pablo Neruda,   83

6. Legacy of the Invisible Man,   110

Notes,   117

Suggested Reading, Including Works Cited,   153

Index,   177

Tribute to Neruda, the poet collector of seashells

Now that I am all but blind,
however it came about,
though I can see as well
as anyone — the imagination

has turned inward as happened
to my mother when she
became old: dreams took the
place of sight. Her native

tongue was Spanish which,
of course, she
never forgot. It was the
language also of Neruda the

Chilean poet — who collected
seashells on his
native beaches, until he
had by reputation, the second

largest collection in the
world. Be patient with
him, darling mother, the
changeless beauty of

seashells, like the
sea itself, gave
his lines the variable pitch
which modern verse requires.

a poetry of things

Are we, perhaps, here just for saying: House, Bridge, Fountain, Gate, Jug, Olive tree, Window, — possibly: Pillar, Tower?[1]

Many a poet writing after the turn of this century is like the man in Virginia Woolf's story "Solid Objects," who, dazzled by the mysterious significance of a piece of green glass that he finds on the beach, turns from the uneasy world of human institutions to the world of things. He finds that he must re-establish contact with what he knows but has forgotten as, waking from a nightmare, "one turns on the light and lies worshipping the chest of drawers, worshipping solidity, worshipping the impersonal world which is a proof of some existence other than ours," says one critic. "That is what one must be sure of."[2]

This experience is shared by four poets who write in the wake of Imagism and Symbolism but not in the militant context of a literary movement. They are William Carlos Williams and Pablo Neruda in the Americas, and Rainer Maria Rilke and Francis Ponge in Europe. These have all written poetry based on the careful examination of concrete things: "It is well, at certain hours of the day and night, to look closely at the world of objects at rest," says Neruda. "From them flow the contacts of man with the earth, like a text for all harassed lyricists. . . . Let that be the poetry we search for."[3] To examine the poetry of things, I call upon these poets who, in their letters and essays, talk about what they try to do. Here I let them speak primarily on the points where they agree, for I am less interested in a comparison of individuals than in the ideas that unite them.

The *Ding*-poets want to remake your world by destroying the stereotyped modes of thinking and seeing that prevent you from knowing it. Their ideas can be understood by turning, as their immediate predecessors did, to Bergson, who explores them more completely than the poets themselves did. Bergson maintains that in ordinary perception we do not see this tree or this flower but *a* tree, *a* flower. Because we classify things according to the use we shall make of them, we see only this classification and not the things themselves. The artist is one who has freed himself from the molds that language and a life of action try to force on human vision, and therefore we say he sees things as they are. The *Ding*-poet does not make up a new world; he shows you the old one. "I speak of things that exist," writes Neruda. "God forbid/ my inventing things when I am singing!" [4]

These poets assume that concrete things bind us together more closely than our ideas about them do. When Williams says that the poet shows the universal in the particular, his "universal" is a particular thing presented by someone who knows what he sees, not sees what he knows. If the poet can keep himself "objective enough, sensual enough," he can, says Williams, produce the factors by which others "shall understand . . . their own world *differing as it may* from mine." [5] To do this, he turns away from himself and from the ideas human beings lay upon things to the things themselves. For he sees that trees and flowers do not change, regardless of the ways we talk about them. "I have no time . . . to waste on ontology," says Ponge, "while I do not have enough time to study objects, to remake them, drawing from them their qualities and delights." [6]

The poet who wants to go back to things believes there are ways of writing about them that he should avoid. First, he distrusts the false unity of what John Crowe Ransom calls Platonic poetry, that is, poetry in which ideas have been linked to things for reasons extraneous to a simple perception of them. According to this belief, the Platonic poet deludes you into thinking you can possess things by reason alone, when you have only made them conform to your ideas about them and revealed nothing of the things themselves. To the *Ding*-poet, all a priori systems of thought make a false unity because they leave out the total richness of the concrete. "It isn't unity that I look for but variety," says Ponge.[7] To write about things, you must leave what Rilke describes as the efficient carriages of systematic thought and walk in the fields to discover, as Williams does over and over, that there are no ideas but in things. This does not mean no ideas should appear in poetry. It means only that they must not appear arsenaled as in a textbook but must be part of the way you see the object itself. Ideas are not stated but implied.

Not only must the *Ding*-poet free his work from ideas that did not come from the things themselves; he must free it from all traces of his own personality. Paul Valéry's definition of the poem as a machine in "Poésie et pensée abstraite,"[8] T. S. Eliot's of the poet as a medium in "Tradition and the Individual Talent,"[9] the Imagists' "doctrine of the image" as described by Ezra Pound[10] — all agree that art comes from an anonymous center. The poet is like Neruda's *hombre invisible*, who gives up his own identity to sing more faithfully the joys and sorrows of others. Just as the surgeon does not feel the cuts he makes, says Williams, so the poet does not let his own circumstances color his observations. He does not shape feelings but things he has felt. To a young poet Rilke writes:

> What you have put out as a craftsman . . . should be a shaping, . . . to which your "ego" was only the first and last impetus, but which from there on remains standing across from you, originating from your impulse but at once removed so far from you to the level of artistic estrangement, of thing-like solitude, that you feel your part in the completion of this mysteriously

objective thing to be but that of a person calmly carrying out some order.[11]

If you want to write of an apple, Rilke continues, do not say, I love; say, here it is. Let your love be consumed without residue in the act of creation. Ponge adds, "I will have realized it better, if I have made a text which has a reality in the world of texts, somewhat equal to that of the apple in the world of objects." [12] The *Ding*-poet sees himself as one who loses his life by making things, "objects, realities which he has to abandon to make another, and another —" says Williams, "perfectly blank to him as soon as they are completed." [13]

The poet is like a *Handwerker*. In "Der Goldschmiedt" ("The Goldsmith"), Rilke calls him the goldsmith whose work translates his own perfections into the life of stones and gold. You do not ask the goldsmith to give you abstract ideas; why, then, should you ask them of the poet? Let poetry be as necessary as bread and water, says Neruda, and let poems stand like cups and tools among the things of this world. Rilke's systematic method for composing many of the *New Poems* (*Neue Gedichte*) — he listed his subjects and dated them as he finished the poems — testifies to his belief at this time that a poet may carry the objectivity of the *Handwerker* into the very processes of poetic creation and attain "the daily madness" (*la frénésie journalière*) of Baudelaire. Williams calls the poet an engineer who designs a machine in which the words are blocks and the spaces are mortar; he seems to believe that the poet can make what Valéry suggests in theory: "a kind of machine for producing the poetic state of mind by means of words." [14]

With what envy Rilke watched his friend Rodin make things that stood free of his personal experiences. And Williams admits that under different circumstances he might have become a painter, but that becoming a poet was the way life arranged it. Often when he writes of his poetic aims, he uses the language of painting. Like a still-life painter, he wants to make you forget that things are useful. An apple or a conversation that he has made into a poem must have no more purpose than "the roundness and the color and the repetition of grapes in a bunch, such grapes as those of Juan Gris which are related more to a ship at sea than to the human tongue." [15] Rilke calls this *Dingwerdung*; the thing has been lifted from the natural world to the orderly world of art. Ponge and Wallace Stevens also understood very well the way of doing this. Ponge's "The Shrimp in All Its States" (*La Crevette dans tous ses états*) and "The Sun of the Abyss" (*Le Soleil placé en abîme*) and Stevens' "Thirteen Ways of Looking at a Blackbird" and "Sea Surface Full of Clouds" are, like so many of their poems, studies in perspective that try to make you see these things as if you had never seen them. The artist "must for subtlety ascend to a plane of almost abstract design to keep alive," says Williams. "Yet what actually impinges on the senses must be rendered as it appears." [16]

Although the *Ding*-poet may envy the painter or sculptor, he never imitates the other arts in the medium of his own. As Lou Andreas-Salomé warned Rilke, "Words do not build like stones, real and concrete things; they are symbols rather for indirectly transmitted suggestions and in themselves far poorer, less substantial than a stone." [17] He may write of Greek sculptures and admire the well-seen apples of Cézanne, but he knows that for himself it is a question of making a text that resembles an apple, that will have as much reality as an apple in its own genre. Yet where the Imagists, Pound, and Valéry thought that language alone could make an objective poem, the *Ding*-poets writing after them seek a special encounter with things, on which the words depend.

To understand this encounter, you must have felt the inexhaustible variety in particular things. Ponge says he cannot imagine trying to realize in words more than the simplest things: stone, grass, fire, wood, meat. He knows this whenever he breaks through utilitarian categories and comes to things in ignorance. Neruda calls for knowledge without antecedent, a physical absorption of himself in the world around him. The *Ding*-poet knows that the man who has made contact with the sensual world is not the man who thinks "hard as a stone" or "black as a panther." He is the one who resists an imposed arrangement of a thing's qualities that fails to reveal its uniqueness. Only when he goes forth as the equal of things and not as their superior can he understand that to see truly is not to arrange them beforehand. Says Ponge: "It is necessary for things to disarrange you." [18]

Ponge proposes a new genre, "definition-descriptions, esthetically and rhetorically satisfying," [19] that will show things as they are by showing the life that unites their particular qualities. Thus, while a single metaphor is one of Rilke's *Dinggedichte*, or while Neruda's elemental odes may show you what it means to be a cat, an elephant, or a flower, Ponge's labored descriptions in such a work as *The Notebook of the Pine Grove* (*Le Carnet du bois de pins*) [20] appear at first sight to be a collection of drafts toward a final utterance not yet achieved. Indeed, Ponge considers many of his poems as approximations, or, at best, tunnels hewn out of rock, rather than positive constructions like buildings or statues. But who is to say that Neruda's panther is more real than Rilke's? That Marianne Moore's snail is false and Ponge's true? That Williams' roses are more accurate than Rilke's? They are all written out of the faith that these things must be seen again in their own country, that the poet sees both people and things as if they were unfamiliar to him. "For men only began to understand Nature when they no longer understood it," says Rilke, "when they felt that it was the Other, indifferent towards men." [21] The *Ding*-poets are really finishing the task the Romantics set for themselves a century earlier, with this difference, implicit in an observation of Wordsworth's:

> The ability to observe with accuracy things as they are in themselves, and with fidelity to describe them, unmodified by any passion or feeling existing in the mind of the describer . . . though indispensable to a Poet, is one which he employs only in submission to necessity, and never for a continuance of time: as its exercise sup-

poses all the higher qualities of the mind to be passive, and in a state of subjection to external objects.[22]

The man for whom external objects are significant only when they show him how the human mind associates ideas in a state of excitement does not recognize the emotion that creates, for example, Ponge's description of water:

It is white and brilliant, formless and fresh, passive and obstinate in its only fault: its weightiness, and it draws upon exceptional means to counter this fault: twisting, transpiercing, eroding, filtering.[23]

But although the *Ding*-poets write about things in different ways, they all start from the moment when the thing rejoices and shows you, says Ponge, a kind of flowering: *le mot juste*. This experience asks of the poet a special kind of sympathy which Rilke calls *Einfühlung*. The opposite of *Einfühlung* is inspection. To inspect a panther means to see it as a window on humanity. But when you feel your way into the nature of the animal, you touch the place from where it begins to be a panther. The object asks, "Are you free? Are you ready to dedicate your whole love to me?"[24] And the poet responds with a love that is not possession but consent; he adapts himself to the thing. To have a thing speak to you, says Rilke, you must approach it as the only thing that exists. Only then will it cry out for expression. "Everyone speaks to me," Neruda exclaims; "they want to tell me things."

Now the universe you see belongs to the *Dinge*. You find yourself with the object in an undivided space that encompasses you both. Rilke calls it *das Offene*. This is where animals and children live who do not understand the divisions of time the civilized world lives by. He describes human consciousness as a pyramid, at the base of which you experience *das Offene*, the unbroken presentness and coming together of everything that, at the upper normal level of self-consciousness, you experience as sequence. For the creature that lives in *das Offene*, being is

> . . . infinite, inapprehensible,
> unintrospective, pure, like its outward gaze.
> Where we see Future, it sees Everything,
> itself in Everything, for ever healed.[26]

Rilke shows how the *Ding* "flowers" for the poet:

"The Mountain" (*Der Berg*)

> SIX-AND-THIRTY and a hundred times
> did the painter write the mountain peak,
> sundered from it, driven back to seek
> (six-and-thirty and a hundred times)
>
> that incomprehensible volcano,
> happy, full of trial, expedientless, —
> while, forever outlined, it would lay no
> bridle on its surging gloriousness:
>
> daily in a thousand ways uprearing,
> letting each incomparable night
> fall away, as being all too tight;
> wearing out at once each new appearing,
> every shape assumed the shiningmost,
> far, opinionless, unsympathising, —
> to be suddenly materialising
> there behind each crevice like a ghost.[27]

Here the artist tries to crack the rigid mask the mountain turns to him. But the rigidity is not in the mountain, any more than is the change in its appearance. Both the rigidity and the revelation are in the artist, who must mend the gap between what the eye sees and the mind knows. Trapped in the static images that his mind gives him, he can only wait for what Williams calls "that happy time when the image becomes broken or begins to break up, becomes a little fluid."[28] Then all his separate impressions coalesce into one, indivisible, having no meaning apart from its own untranslatable concreteness. The mountain radiates into the poet's consciousness, so that his knowledge of it is absolute, for it is relative to no particular impression and it includes all of them. "Truth is not the conclusion of a system," says Ponge; "truth is simply that." [29]

Rilke, Ponge, and Williams compare this kind of perception to falling asleep. Williams sees sleep as his release from the concentric layers of self-interest that prevent him from moving into the lives of others. "I lost myself in the very properties of their minds. . . . For the moment . . . nothing of myself affected me," he writes of his attitude toward his patients, which he carries into his poetry; "it was as though I were reawakening from a sleep." [30] Neruda, too, wants a physical absorption of himself into things.

For the European poets, the enchanted sleep silences not only the ego but the senses as well. Insights, images, and impressions must be lost to the senses in order to be changed. Williams writes of the girl he sees; Rilke, wanting to show the beauty of the particular girl in *Sonnets to Orpheus* (*Die Sonette an Orpheus*), must first forget her. She must fall asleep inside him and be changed by long contact with his thoughts, feelings, and insights. To examine the processes of her transformation would destroy them. All he can know is that the most insignificant things — bells that suddenly cease ringing, a glance from a window — may be the innocent confederates of the imagination that will awaken her. But she will awaken only if the poet is already prepared for the surrender of himself that is necessary for her reappearance. It is less a question of knowing, says Ponge, than of being born.

What the *Ding*-poet celebrates in the poem is nothing less than everything. No subject is "antipoetic." Both Williams and Ponge use this term; yet Williams dislikes it because it implies a division in the sensual world that has no basis in experience. Man forgets, says Rilke, how innocently things happen in Nature. "Her consciousness consists in her completeness," he writes: "because she contains *everything*, she contains the cruel too." [31] Neruda also demands that the new poetry be as impure as the clothes we wear, permeated with sweat and smoke, smelling of urine and lilies, spattered by the various trades that we live by, inside the law or beyond it. For art is not a selection from the world but a transformation of it into something that praises existence.

> Give me all the sorrow
> of everyone,

says Neruda;

> I am going to transform it
> into hope.[32]

If the poet fails, says Williams, he fails through his own lack of power, not through his material.

These poets believe that at the heart of all failures to see is an unwillingness to remain without answers, even when you are faced with contradictions that make action impossible until they are resolved. To the poet whose own existence excludes nothing, it seems that man has had to deny whatever does not fit into his systems of thought, in order for the human-centered world to operate most efficiently. The most insidious of these denials, to the *Ding*-poet, is Christianity, because it shifts our responsibility from this world to one unknown to us and passes judgment on what is innocent. "The view that one is sinful and needs ransom as premise for God," says Rilke, "is more and more repugnant to a heart that has comprehended the earth." [33]

Particularly in the *Duino Elegies* and *The Notebooks of Malte Laurids Brigge* (*Die Aufzeichnungen des Malte Laurids Brigge*), Rilke shows how man denies his past to manipulate the present and create for himself a space in which he can act. He makes death the Outside and Other (*Anderwärtiges und Anderes*) to justify his own mortality. Then he finds that action is indeed possible but at a price: The present becomes a series of disconnected snapshots without order and without meaning. The radiance and song that might have arisen from the very mortality he refuses to accept have been delivered over to a promise, a Jerusalem to be inhabited later. The superficial centers of Ponge's *pseudo-civilization*, Rilke's City of Pain (*Leid*-

Stadt), and Neruda's betrayed arena (*Arena Traicionada*) are responsible for the problems at their surfaces.

All four writers agree that before the poet can see things as they are, he must break down the answers he has lived by in the past and return to his life all that he has pushed out. His poems should not preserve his values but destroy them at the moment of their discovery, before they begin to look like laws. When you know how to destroy your ideas as well as how to construct them, then, says Ponge, you are ready to be saved. You will find your law and your god within yourself. Your viewpoint must be so broad that even contradictions can exist harmoniously together. "All art is this: love, which has been poured out over enigmas — " observes Rilke, "and all works of art are enigmas surrounded, adorned, enveloped by love." [34] Only in *das Offene* is such harmony possible. There the past survives and flows into the present, as indivisibly joined as the notes of a melody. And death no longer stands outside but appears, says Rilke, as a silent and necessary participant in everything alive.

But none of this can happen until the old person dies for the sake of a new one. This is the crisis that Sartre describes so well in *Nausea* (*La Nausée*), when even a chestnut root suddenly loses the harmless look of an abstract category: "The words had vanished and with them the significance of things, their methods of use, and the feeble points of reference which men have traced on their surface." [35] Neruda, too, in "Ritual of My Legs" (*Ritual de mis piernas*), finds that things confront him like a wall of nameless unities, alien and hostile. The world he understands ends at his own feet.

The crisis breaks out when you cling to an order that your experience constantly tells you is false. Rilke's hero in *The Notebooks of Malte Laurids Brigge* survives only as long as he believes in the comfortable boundaries of human habit. When his faith in this order collapses, Malte, denying the reality of his past, also loses his future. He finds himself confronting the naked, unnamable existence of things. *La Nausée* describes Malte's experience as well as Sartre's: "Suddenly they existed, then suddenly they existed no longer," writes Sartre; "existence is without memory; of the vanished it retains nothing — not even a memory." [36] Neruda lays bare the terrors of this experience in *Residence on Earth* (*Residencia en la tierra*) and plunges into a dislocated world where everything gallops helplessly toward death. You only begin to understand nature, says Rilke, when you think you do not, when you feel its indifference toward you.

To see things as they are, you must both see them and say them. For the *Ding*-poet, expression is knowledge. Everything is words, says Ponge. Therefore to say that one will leave words and go to things is false. "Taking the side of things *equals* making allowances for words." [37] But language conceals the nuances of things rather than reveals them. Writing against the failures of the spoken word, Ponge even insists, as did Valéry before him, that speaking and writing are contrary to one another.

The *Ding*-poets restore words to their original colors by bringing them close to things. They work against a tendency in human thought to abstract the qualities that things have in common. To use Pound's example, you say that a flamingo is red, when you know quite well that the flamingo is not red, but rather the flamingo is what it does. In an essay on the Chinese written character, Pound describes language as a pyramid of ascending abstractions, moving away from the concrete world toward the apex "being." At the bottom lie the things, stunned, that can never know themselves unless they pass up and down the layers of the pyramid.[38] The poet must save them from the pyramid; he must find, says Ponge, a rhetoric of things.

A rhetoric of things as these poets see it works in two ways. For the American writers it means giving the senses new currency. For we must never forget, says Williams, "that we smell, hear and see with words and words alone, and that with a new language we smell, hear and see afresh." [39] And while both Williams and Neruda reject the lack of preciseness in the spoken language, they nevertheless base a new prosody on the rhythms of speech. Neruda wants to write for everyone, including the most ignorant peasant, by writing in the language that everyone understands.

The American poets feel, too, that it is not enough to renew man's vision of things; they want to break down his isolation by renewing his vision of himself. It starts, says Williams, with a conversation or a remark heard in passing that reveals the secret twist of a whole people's way of thinking, "the poem which their lives are being lived to realize." It is man himself, "inarticulate for the most part except when in the poem one man, every five or six hundred years, escapes to formulate a few gifted sentences." [40] The need for expression starts with men and women whose lives cry out for the poet to make conversation possible again.

For the European poets, however, the rhetoric of things is not the language of Neruda and Williams and Pound but the rhetoric of revelation, as it was for Mallarmé. The poet is not a listener in the world of human experience but the lonely one who withdraws to his great inner solitude. And Ponge declares that poets need not concern themselves with their human relationships; they are the ambassadors of the silent world. Like Zarathustra, the poet-prophet names things in the new dimension in which he has come to perceive them:

> Here the words and word-shrines of everything that is, open up before me; everything that is, wishes to become word; everything that will become, wishes to learn from me how to speak.[41]

The word becomes the Word and the poet the god who utters it. "The Word is God," cries Ponge. "I am the Word!" [42]

Only the poet can speak so lovingly that the *Dinge* are touched and open like flowers at his call. He is, says Rilke, a magician, whose word gives life. The word grows mysteriously beyond the range of his own faculties, to awaken the things that wait in silence, like a lute whose melodies wait for the touch of strings. "Taking the side of things" means this sensitivity to the plight of things that wait for us to give them expression. It is, Ponge tells us, the feeling that nothing has been said properly, a conviction that also causes Malte to ask himself if it is possible that nothing real has been said or done in the world and to answer, it is possible.

Both the poet who withdraws from human experience and the poet who affirms it have a common aim, the reconciliation of the Individual and the All. He may take the side of things, but he never forgets that the poem is, as Ponge describes it, an object of joy proposed for man and only for him. For it is not things that speak among themselves but men who speak of things among themselves. And the poet, in putting man among things, recognizes that he too is as mute as the fish or the stone. When he speaks he utters nothings that express only his isolation. Contrary to the ideas of the early Symbolists, the *Ding*-poet believes that Nature, including man, is a *nonsignificative* writing; that is, it refers to no system of signification and therefore demands expression.

The order that he celebrates is as brittle and crumbling as the things themselves. He is, says Ponge, the attentive restorer of the lobster or the lemon, the pitcher or the dish. In his ninth *Duino Elegy* (*Die neunte Elegie*), Rilke writes:

For the wanderer doesn't bring from the mountain slope
a handful of earth to the valley, untellable earth, but only
some word he has won, a pure word, the yellow and blue
gentian. Are we, perhaps, here just for saying: House,
Bridge, Fountain, Gate, Jug, Olive tree, Window, —
possibly: Pillar, Tower? . . . but for saying, remember,
oh, for such saying as never the things themselves
hoped so intensely to be.[48]

The impermanence of things makes them both beautiful and terrible, like two faces on a single head: the face it shows depends on who looks at it. The poet offers no eter-

nal rest and no answers, but rather a way of marching in
step with time, like the steed and the rider, soon to be sepa-
rated by pasture and table:

> But let us now be glad a while
> to believe the figure. That's enough.[44]

chapter 2

a local habitation:
william carlos williams

> — Say it, no ideas but in things —
> nothing but the blank faces of the houses
> and cylindrical trees
> bent, forked by preconception and accident —
> split, furrowed, creased, mottled, stained —
> secret — into the body of the light! [1]

The business of poetry, says William Carlos Williams, is to show the universal in the local. The universal is a particular thing, pointed out by someone who has freed himself from the self-interest that prevents people from seeing what they already know. It is, says Dewey, whose influence Williams admits, "not something metaphysically anterior to all experience but is a *way in which things function* in experience as a bond of union among particular events and scenes." [2] Williams means something very close to this:

> Being an artist I can produce, if I am able, universals of general applicability. If I succeed in keeping myself objective enough, sensual enough, I can produce the factors, the concretions of materials by which others shall understand and so be led to use — that they may the better see, touch, taste, enjoy — their own world *differing as it may from mine.* . . .
>
> That — all my life I have striven to emphasize it — is what is meant by the universality of the local. From me where I stand to them where they stand in their

here and now — where I cannot be — I do in spite of
that arrive! ³

By showing you his experience, he shows you yours.

Williams talks about particular things in two ways.
First, he means the physical presence of people and things,
made into images, for whatever is well seen, he says, becomes sight and song itself. But as he continues to write and
to move further away from his early Imagist position, he
recognizes that not everything worth writing about can be
made into images. In *Paterson* he says that he is seeking the
"Beautiful Thing." Trying to name what cannot be named
apart from the moment when it happens, he calls it a "rare
presence," "a rarest element," "that essence which is hidden
in the very words which are going in at our ears." ⁴ It is,
says Williams, the perfect articulation, however fragmen-
tary, of what man everywhere thinks and feels. Images let
you see the particular. But the "rare presence" is something
you hear in the language itself. When Williams discusses
the particular as both the image seen and the words heard,
his ideas are sometimes ambiguous.

Williams writes about things because he knows that
they are important, that sparrows, chimneys, rotten apples,
daisies, and an old woman eating plums are worth his attention. When his poems work, the reader knows this too, as,
for example in "Sea-Trout and Butterfish":

> The contours and the shine
> hold the eye — caught and lying
>
> orange-finned and the two
> half its size, pout-mouthed
>
> beside it on the white dish —
> Silver scales, the weight
>
> quick tails
> whipping the streams aslant
>
> The eye comes down eagerly
> unravelled of the sea

> separates this from that
> and the fine fins' sharp spines [5]

Like the Imagists here, Williams uses static images rather than the fluid, metaphorical, and highly subjective imagery of Pound. He admits that he thought of many of his early poems as still lifes and studies in observation. "To me, at that time, a poem was an image, the picture was the important thing," he says.[6] More than any other Imagist poet, however, Williams resembles a painter in his way of seeing things, and he says, "You must remember I had a strong inclination all my life to be a painter. Under different circumstances I would rather have been a painter than to bother with these god-damn words. . . . Becoming a poet was the way life arranged it." [7]

Williams' poems are not word-paintings. As he studies the scene, he watches his own eye bring together both the sense of movement implied in the "quick tails/whipping the streams" and the sense of stillness as he leisurely separates part from part. He savors the process of discovering color and form, and he implies the value of his subject in the way he presents it. In another image-poem, he praises it directly:

> so much depends
> upon
>
> a red wheel
> barrow
>
> glazed with rain
> water
>
> beside the white
> chickens. (*CEP*, 277)

But Williams wants to do more than make images. He wants to set down both the thing and his response to it. "The world of the senses lies unintelligible on all sides," he says. "It only exists when its emotion is fastened to it." [8] This emotion is not personal; it comes from a detached con-

templation of the thing itself. Williams believes that the
sentimental or associational value of things is the false one.
"A poet witnessing the chicory flower and realizing its vir-
tues of form and color so constructs his praise of it as to bor-
row no particle from right or left," he says.[9] The poem
"says" nothing more than this. Thus, of the chicory, he
writes:

> Lift your flowers
> on bitter stems
> chicory!
> Lift them up
> out of the scorched ground!
> Bear no foliage
> but give yourself
> wholly to that!
> Strain under them
> you bitter stems
> that no beast eats —
> and scorn greyness!
> Into the heat with them:
> cool!
> luxuriant! sky-blue!
> The earth cracks and
> is shriveled up;
> the wind moans piteously;
> the sky goes out
> if you should fail. (*CEP*, 122)

Williams might have said "so much depends" on
flowers that flourish in the most unfertile places, bitter and
scorned, for they are necessary to his world, and must be included in a celebration of it. Toward nature he is passion-
ate "but not assertive; I have always believed in keeping
myself out of the picture." When he writes of flowers, he
says he *is* a flower, "with all the prerogatives of flowers,
especially the right to come alive in the Spring." [10] This respect for the thing itself, not merely his impression of it,

lets Williams sustain long, densely descriptive poems in a way that the Imagists could not.

The local environment out of which Williams shapes his poems comes in at the ear as well as the eye. *"What do I do?"* says the poet in *Paterson*, Book II, *"I listen. . . . This is my entire occupation"* (p. 60). Williams tells us that the object of his listening is not simply words but what is embedded in words. "We can't name it," says Williams; "we know it never gets into any recognizable avenue of expression." He describes it as "that essence which is hidden in the very words which are going in at our ears"; it is sure, it is there, and it vanishes. It is the expression that reveals the secret twist of a whole community's way of thinking and living, the poem their lives are being lived to realize. It wears a particular face on each of its appearances and never the same one twice. "It is we ourselves, at our rarest moments, but inarticulate for the most part except when in the poem one man, every five or six hundred years, escapes to formulate a few gifted sentences." [11] Sometimes Williams jots down the words as he hears them and lets them stand alone. At other times he has to revise them to bring out what he heard there. But his aim is always the same:

> The poem springs from the half-spoken words of such patients as the physician sees from day to day. He observes it in the peculiar, actual conformations in which its life is hid. Humbly he presents himself before it and by long practice he strives as best he can to interpret the manner of its speech. In that the secret lies. This, in the end, comes perhaps to be the occupation of the physician after a lifetime of careful listening. [12]

Since he wants to show people to themselves, Williams fights all stereotyped forms of communication that reduce human behavior to rules, formulas, or statistics. No one sees the importance of particular things so well as a doctor. "Whole lives are spent in the tremendous affairs of daily events without even approaching the great sights that I see every day." [13] Selection lies in the poet's sensitivity to what it tells him about human life. "By listening to the minutest variations of the speech," says Williams, "we begin to detect that today, as always, the essence is also to be found, hidden under the verbiage, seeking to be realized." [14]

Williams knows that he must shape his experiences if he is to recover the metal from the ore; at the same time, he distrusts the intellectual revision of authentic material. Of the people whose speech he tries to bring into his poems, he writes:

> They were perfect, they seem to have been born perfect, to need nothing else. They were there, living before me. . . . Their very presence denied the need of "study," that is study by degrees to elucidate them. They were, living, the theme that all my life I have labored to elucidate, and when I could not elucidate them I have tried to put them down, to lay them upon the paper to record them: for to do that is, after all, a sort of elucidation. [15]

When Williams follows his own advice to the letter, he writes such snatches of realism as "Detail":

> Doc, I bin lookin' for you
> I owe you two bucks.
>
> How you doin'?
>
> Fine. When I get it
> I'll bring it up to you. (*CEP*, 427)

But here neither the underlying essence is clear nor the sense of form that makes speech into poetry. The actual words are not enough. This does not mean that the poet must give up the idiom of speech. A poem made up entirely of local expressions can still be universal if those expressions are part of a poetic structure, as they are in "Shoot it Jimmy!"

> Our orchestra
> is the cat's nuts —
>
> Banjo jazz
> with a nickelplated

amplifier to
soothe

the savage beast —
Get the Rhythm

That sheet stuff
's a lot a cheese.

Man
gimme the key

and lemme loose —
I make 'em crazy

with my harmonies —
Shoot it Jimmy

Nobody
Nobody else

but me —
They can't copy it. (*CEP*, 269)

Williams claims that his main problem in writing poetry has always been to find a form for what has none. Here
he lets a jazz musician speak for himself. Yet Williams does
more than set down the actual words. He makes them his
own in order to bring out their original enthusiasm and
humor. Although poetry starts with the actual world, Williams knows that it occupies a place outside of nature. It is,
he tells us, an imitation of nature, a re-creation of an event
in the language appropriate to it. When Williams speaks of
the essence which the poem communicates, he says that
means "compact, restricted to essentials. . . . The essence
remains in the parts proper to life, in all their sensual
reality." [16]

Yet often what Williams actually heard is either too
imprecise or too brief to be a poem by itself. Struck by the
pathos of a single remark, such as "I won't have any more"
or "I can't die," Williams gives it a particular context. In

"To an Old Jaundiced Woman," he evokes the setting with sparse but moving details:

> O tongue
> licking
> the sore on
> her netherlip
>
> O toppled belly
>
> O passionate cotton
> stuck with
> matted hair
>
> elsian slobber
> upon
> the folded handkerchief
>
> I can't die
>
> — moaned the old
> jaundiced woman
> rolling her
> saffron eyeballs
>
> I can't die
> I can't die. (*CEP*, 268)

The woman's speech does not give you the details; yet they are important to its impact. They let you see the person whose pathetic exclamation is the plight of the sick and the old. Williams the listener listens for statements such as this one. But he also listens for a language under the spoken language, whose meaning is clumsily conveyed by the words going in at his ears. This is not symbolism; it is only Williams' way of saying that the poet may articulate an emotion more clearly than the subject himself is able to do. The poet's language is free of localisms, as simple and intense as that of the anonymous fifteenth-century song writers to whom Williams has been compared. Few of his poems show this transformation from actual speech to a more expressive medium better than "The Widow's Lament in Springtime":

> Sorrow is my own yard
> where the new grass
> flames as it has flamed
> often before but not
> with the cold fire
> that closes round me this year.
> Thirtyfive years
> I lived with my husband.
> The plumtree is white today
> with masses of flowers.
> Masses of flowers
> load the cherry branches
> and color some bushes
> yellow and some red
> but the grief in my heart
> is stronger than they
> for though they were my joy
> formerly, today I notice them
> and turned away forgetting.
> Today my son told me
> that in the meadows,
> at the edge of the heavy woods
> in the distance, he saw
> trees of white flowers.
> I feel that I would like
> to go there
> and fall into those flowers
> and sink into the marsh near them. (*CEP*, 223)

Williams has said that the aim of writing is to reveal what is inside a man; he accepts "stream of consciousness" as a means of transforming the actual language into one more significant. In "The Widow's Lament," Williams' choice of metaphors as well as his speaker's consciousness order the details. The new grass is a cold fire; its vitality only emphasizes her grief. The poem shifts from perception to statement, from the flowers whose fullness and life are too rich for her, to her son's observation, suggested by the flowers, and at last to her wish for death. Williams assumes a voice that is neither his own nor the one that he heard, but rather the voice that he senses behind the actual words and that he tries to re-create.

In much of his writing about his own verse, Williams tries to defend its form — or lack of it. He feels that traditional forms would not only falsify his perceptions but would actually restrict the content of his poems. When a poetic form is born, it flowers briefly, then calcifies, and if it is not changed, it causes a stasis in poetic thought by limiting the means of expression. For Williams there is no theoretical poetic form, no grammar of poetry. There is only poetry.

Williams' search for form begins with the search for new laws of metrics. Because he wants to keep the rhythms of actual speech, he wants a measure that will clarify the authentic material from which his poems are made. He says that there is no such thing as free verse except as a transitional phase. Free verse is poetry to which ordinary laws of prosody cannot be applied, for they are incomplete experiments in the direction of a new measure.

Listening to the rhythms of speech, he tries to find a variable meter, based on the rhythms of spoken prose similar to that which the Imagists described. And just as the Imagists acknowledged no difference in kind between poetry and prose, so Williams believes that poetry and prose belong together. The letters, lists, and newspaper anecdotes sprinkled throughout *Paterson*, for example, are, he feels, formally justified by their context. He wants a new measure elastic enough to fit actual speech; yet he recognizes the need for a standard which will make departures from it effective. "The line must, as a minimum, have a well-conceived form within which modification may exist," he says. "Without this internal play upon the stops, it cannot achieve power." [17] He seems to ask of measure that it include all potential irregularities.

Williams' solution to these problems is the *variable foot*, a three-stress line at which he arrives only when he tries to describe the unconscious order in his own work. In an early book, *The Tempers* (1913), he is already beginning to reject conventional punctuation and rhyme so that he can be more faithful to the spoken word. From 1917 into the 1930's he is more concerned with the image than with form, but his inability to describe the form of his own work continues to trouble him, up to the writing of *Paterson* in 1946, at which time he decides, with a nonchalance that is typical of him, simply to reject the problem altogether. "Finally I let form take care of itself; the colloquial language, my own language, set the pace," he writes. "Once in a while I would worry but I put my worries aside." [18]

Finding no measure in verse as he wanted to write it, Williams turned briefly to free verse in 1953 and defended it as enthusiastically as he had rejected it earlier. Then, quite by accident, he tells us, as he was reading a section from *Paterson*, Book III, several years after he had written it, he found the measure that he had sought in his own verse for so long:

> I realized I had hit upon a device (that is the practical focus of a device) which I could not name when I wrote it. My dissatisfaction with free verse came to a head in that I always wanted a verse that was ordered, so it came to me that the concept of the foot itself would have to be altered. . . . I had a feeling that there was somewhere an exact way to define it; the task was to find the word to describe it, to give it an epitaph, and I finally hit upon it. The foot not being fixed is only to be described as variable. . . . Thus the verse becomes not free at all but just simply variable, as all things in life properly are. [19]

Williams' method of discovering the variable foot makes it of questionable value for judging his poetry. It justifies work already composed; it does not grow out of a conscious experimentation in metrics. A count of the regular beats in any line of a poem by Williams does not really help you to understand it. Although his lines often do contain a regular number of beats, the variation in secondary accents keeps his rhythms from ever falling into traditional meter. The spontaneous, accidental nature of Williams' methods makes it almost impossible to generalize about them. He admits that the first draft of a poem is often the only draft. The lines, he explains, are unstudied. The poet is one who has stepped beyond measure. He is a maker, not a measurer. "It is that the material is so molded that it is changed in *kind* from other statement," he writes. "It is a *sort* beyond measure." The meter, or rather the movement, is peculiar and unmeasurable.[20]

If you want to talk about form in Williams' poems, you will have to remember that they were written without rules and that the conventional tools of metrical analysis are inappropriate to him. He wanted to emphasize the spoken language of his own time and place and to make his own attitudes toward things implicit in every part of his poems.

Williams can write longer and more sustained poems than he is generally given credit for. In "The Crimson Cyclamen" (*CEP*, 397–404) you find the lively imagery and inseparable joining of thing and idea that you expect in Williams' shorter poems, but the development of both image and idea is more complex. The poem describes a plant's flowering and fading, yet metaphor is so unobtrusively used that you hardly know when he has moved from facts to the interpretation of facts. Williams sees in the cyclamen the supreme fragility of all things that reach a brilliant climax and then rapidly decline. He starts with the actual plant as he sees it, in full bloom.

> White suffused with red
> more rose than crimson
> — all acolor
> the petals flare back
> from the stooping craters
> of those flowers
> as from a wind rising —

And though the light
that enfolds and pierces
them discovers blues
and yellows there also —
and crimson's a dull word
beside such play —
yet the effect against
this winter where
they stand — is crimson —

It is miraculous
that flower should rise
by flower
alike in loveliness —
as though mirrors
of some perfection
could never be
too often shown —
silence holds them
in that space. And
color has been construed
from emptiness
to waken there —

Color is active, something awakened by the play of light in the petals: The white is "suffused" with red; the light "enfolds and pierces" the flowers and "discovers" such colors there that the single word *crimson* cannot show all the nuances in that shade.

Williams' other flower poems also convert color into light and movement. Even such an early one as "Flowers by the Sea" shows this special way of describing them; chicory and daisies, says Williams, "seem hardly flowers alone/ but color and . . . movement." They are to him the shape of restlessness itself (*CEP*, 87). The flowers act, they are not simply observed. In "The Pot of Flowers" (*CEP*, 242) a petal "lays its glow" on other petals; in "The Rose" (*CEP*, 369) you see "A grace of petals skirting/ the tight-whorled cone" with a strong sense of movement implied in *whorled*.

one of Williams' favorite words. Characteristically, color and movement shape his description of the cyclamen.

It is miraculous, says Williams, that perfection should so repeat itself in these flowers. They have nothing to do with the bustle and grind of the human world. Williams circumscribes them with a space that divorces them from all else. Color and light are blossoming; under his gentle gaze, the cyclamen unfolds itself. The leaves, "quirked and green," precede the flowers:

> Upon each leaf it is
> a pattern more
> of logic than a purpose
> links each part to the rest,
> an abstraction
> playfully following
> centripetal
> devices, as of pure thought —
> the edge tying by
> convergent, crazy rays
> with the center —
>
> . . . .
> Such are the leaves
> freakish, of the air
> as thought is, of roots
> dark, complex from
> subterranean revolutions
> . . . . (*CEP*, 398–99).

But this is no longer a poem simply about the life of a plant. The pattern on the leaf, more of logic than of purpose, is as useless as pure thought. The design that splays out and returns upon itself is eccentric, "freakish," as unsubstantial as air. More than the design links the leaves, in Williams' mind, to pure thought. In their fruitless complexity they do not blossom; they endure like that concrete and fixed present where Williams is always alert for a possibility of movement. This fixed design is reason itself. Yet the source of the leaves, which their elegant abstraction tries to

deny, is the roots, hidden and inexplicable. Williams knows
that reason is only part of the whole man, and when it is
isolated, it is inadequate. All the parts of the design

> link together
> the unnicked argument
> to the last crinkled edge —
> where the under and the over
> meet and disappear
> and the air alone begins
> to go from them —
> the conclusion left still
> blunt, floating   (*CEP*, 400).

Thought by itself bears no fruit. The useless perfection
of abstract reasoning and the perfection of the leaves merge
in the metaphor of the unnicked argument. Williams reduces thought to a dead end and turns to the flowers:

> it begins that must
> put thought to rest —
>
> wakes in tinted beaks
> still raising the head
> and passion
> is loosed —   (*CEP*, 400).

This is the escape that Williams lives for, the release
from himself that puts him in touch with the "primitive
profundity of the personality" that is more than the idiosyncrasies of one man. "The faculties, untied, proceed back-
ward through the night of our unconscious past," says Williams, uncovering "the rhythmic ebb and flow of the mysterious life process and unless this is tapped by the writer
nothing of moment can result." [21]

The petals emerge and the flower "flows to release."
Through short stanzas and short lines, he unfolds the ecstasy
of their awakening, the triumph of passion over thought.
For the flowers, says Williams, are:

the frail fruit
by its frailty supreme

opening in the tense moment
to no bean
no completion
no root
no leaf and no stem
but color only and a form —

It is passion
earlier and later than thought
that rises above thought
at instant peril — peril
itself a flower
that lifts and draws it on —

Frailer than level thought
more convolute
rose red
highest
the soonest to wither
blacken
and fall upon itself
formless —   (*CEP*, 402–3).

Now when Williams speaks of passion, he speaks of the flower as well. The flower is supremely useless, like the design on the leaf, but it is a uselessness that Williams admires: beauty whose flowering is as frail and intense as the light that makes time pass in a horizon of colors. It is our own lives we see passing as the flowers age before our eyes and deep veins mark the purity of their color. There is no departure from the concrete for the sake of these ideas. The precise description of particular things found in the best Imagist poetry is here, but there is much more: ideas skillfully implied but never stated except through the description of the cyclamen. Both the ideas in the poem and the way of handling them are peculiarly Williams' own.

Quite different but equally complex is "Two Pendants:

for the Ears, II; Elena." [22] It is more realistic than "The Crimson Cyclamen" in that it uses actual conversation. Yet like that poem, it is also rhetorical, for he uses a more elaborate arrangement of metaphors than is found in normal speech. These styles bring together the actual world of the poet and the imaginative world of his response to it. The poem opens on the imaginative level:

> You lean the head forward
> and wave the hand,
> with a smile,
> twinkling the fingers
>
>> I say to myself
>> Now it is spring
>> Elena is dying
>
> What snows, what snow
> enchained her —
> she of the tropics
> is melted
>> now she is dying
>
> The mango, the guava
> long forgot for
> apple and cherry
> wave good-bye
>> now it is spring
>> Elena is dying
>>> Good-bye   (*CLP*, 220–21).

In this imaginative world, Elena's death is not tragic; her farewell in the poet's mind is as light as if she were going on a journey. It is spring, and the snows are melting; the winter of her sickness is leaving her. But where nature is released for new life by spring, she is released from life by death. This melting loosens her attention from the present and lets the past return briefly, which is for her a tropical background long forgotten, exchanged for life in colder climates. The inner world of her mind and the outer world coincide here. The phrase, "Elena is dying," which becomes "Now she is dying," is set up as a refrain. Williams uses it later to contrast the imaginative world with the actual one.

The next section, approximately four stanzas long, consists of a dialogue between the doctor-poet and the couple taking care of his mother. They discuss her death from a purely physical standpoint and are amazed at her refusal to die.

> Why just an hour ago
> she sat up straight on that bed, as
> straight as ever I saw her
> in the last ten years, straight
> as a ram-rod. You wouldn't believe
> that would you? She's not
> going to die . she'll be
> raising Cain, looking for her grub
> as per usual in the next two
> or three days, you wait and see   (*CLP*, 221).

What was said at the imaginative level is completely reversed; food for Williams is one of the sensual delights that bind us to this life. The shopping list that follows the stanza just quoted, with its exotic variety — trout from Denmark, ducks, partridges, a crab — are his pleasure and praise of it. "What about that?" he asks the others in the poem. The answer comes in the modified refrain, "Elena is dying (I wonder)," and his language shifts back to the imaginative world:

> Elena is dying (I wonder)
> willows and pear trees
> whose encrusted branches
> blossom all a mass
> attend her on her way —
>
> a guerdon
>   (a garden)
>   and cries of children

indeterminate
Holy, holy, holy

(no ritual
but fact . in fact).

until
the end of time (which is now)   (*CLP*, 222).

Williams juxtaposes the hard fact of death with the
Christian escape from death. Since the woman is dying in
the spring, she will be attended by the new blossoms of the
season. The word *mass* describing the blossoms leads to a
pun on the ritual of the Mass and formalized Christianity
with its promise of salvation. This, of course, Williams does
not accept. "Death is too real for me to want to become
'dramatic' about it," he says. "It claps you between its
hands like a flying moth, and you are done; only those who
hope find that tragic." [23] The "guerdon" is a "garden"; the
dying woman's salvation is a return to the earth. The cries
of the children are not cherubic hymns but the accidental
noises of the real world. The end of time for her is not
eternity but the end of her life; only the sensual world is
holy. His grief is for his own loss, not out of fear for her
ultimate salvation. "She will go alone," says Williams, picking up the suggestion of the journey in the opening lines.
She will

go wept
by a clay statuette
(if there be miracles)
a broken head of a small
St. Anne who wept at a kiss
from a child:
She was so lonely   (*CLP*, 223).

If miracles attend her, they are miracles that have happened in his own time and place, in the everyday world.
The subject of the miracle is bantered about by the doctor
and the couple attending the woman. In the midst of their

conversation, Williams injects images that metaphorically comment on her. She is, for example, "The river, throwing off sparks in a cold world," almost extinguished in a world where miracles are doubted, where magazines and newspapers argue over the rights to reveal them, and where conversation, even in the face of death, trails off to trivial relationships, avoiding the woman whose life is, as all life is for Williams, a miracle. The refrain returns to explain the last words of the dying woman:

> Elena is dying.
> In her delirium she said
> a terrible thing:
>
> Who are you? NOW!
> I, I, I, I stammered. I
> am your son.   (*CLP*, 224)

Death brings mother and son together again. Their last conversation, which is both comic and pathetic, recalls "The Last Words of My English Grandmother." As in that poem, the old woman in "Two Pendants: for the Ears" pits her will against those who think they know what is best for her. The poet brings her a bottle of Spanish sherry, and she asks for a glass.

> Has
> she eaten anything yet?
>
> Has
> she eaten anything yet!
>
> Six oysters — she said
> she wanted some fish and that's
> all we had. A round
> of bread and butter and a
> banana
>
> My God!
>
> — two cups of tea and some
> ice-cream.

Now she wants the wine.

Will it hurt her?

No, I think
nothing will hurt her.

She's
one of the wonders of the world
I think, said his wife.   (*CLP*, 227–28)

Her voracious appetite still keeps her in the land of the living, among those who have not yet renounced the things of this world. For Williams, the miracle of her will to live is far more real than the publicized miracle of the weeping St. Anne. "Whole lives are spent in the tremendous affairs of daily events without even approaching the great sights that I see every day." [24]

He knows that when April comes, the waking of new life will only remind him of his loss. Suddenly it seems to him that the canary that comes and sits on the breakfast table is "a smart little bird," for it does not feel the indifference of others in the face of death. But without his awareness of death he could not celebrate life. He sees in this experience the value of all experience:

(To make the language
record it, facet to facet
not bored out —
with an auger.
— to give also the unshaven,
the rumblings of a
catastrophic past, a delicate
defeat — vivid simulations of
the mystery   .   )   (*CLP*, 228)

This poem does what all of his poetry tries to do: It joins his life to the lives around him, which are urgent, mysterious, and beyond judgment.

In "The Mind Hesitant," Williams watches his own mind acting on particular things:

Sometimes the river
becomes a river in the mind
or of the mind
or in and of the mind

Its banks snow
the tide falling a dark
rim lies between
the water and the shore

And the mind hesitant
regarding the stream
senses
a likeness which it

will find — a complex
image: something
of white brows
bound by a ribbon

of sooty thought
beyond, yes well beyond
the mobile features
of swiftly

flowing waters, before
the tide will
change
and rise again, maybe (*CLP*, 118).

The poem describes what Williams has in mind when he says that the artist makes "an other nature." [25] Distinguishing between the river in and of the mind, he describes three possible relationships of the mind to its object. The river exists in nature and the mind sees it; it is remembered or invented, and is of the mind; or it is both: The mind puts itself into the external world and identifies itself with what it finds there. The mind is not merely compared to a river; in this meeting, the river takes on the life of the mind and, in the fourth stanza, becomes a replica of the mind itself.

To see how Williams makes the idea inseparable from the thing here, it is helpful to start with his arrangement of images within each stanza rather than with his metrics. In the first stanza of "The Mind Hesitant" he states all these relationships, making the necessary qualifications through a three-line repetition of the phrase "in (of, in and of) the mind." He follows immediately with details of the river whose transformation he will show later: the banks white with snow, the tide, the rim between water and shore. In the third stanza he returns to the real subject of the poem: the mind, which identifies itself with the river and joins the separate parts set out in stanza two into a "complex image"

> of white brows
> bound by a ribbon
>
> of sooty thought
> beyond, yes well beyond
> the mobile features
> of swiftly
>
> flowing waters . . .   (*CLP*, 118).

The landscape of the poem becomes both the thinker who is seen and his thoughts that lie under the surface of his speech. The metaphor of water for the mind is one of Williams' favorites. The real language of men, he says in *The Autobiography*, is an underground stream that sometimes comes to the surface; and when he deals with the failure of language in *Paterson*, he chooses the image of a waterfall. Yet the particular thing that carries the idea never blurs into a symbol, not even, as in the stanza quoted above, when the river has been completely transformed into a replica of the mind. The water's tides are certain and will surely change; the tides of the mind hesitant will "rise again, maybe," and uncover briefly what is hidden there.

What is hidden there has its own value, the value of the past, which has little to do with personal memories. To Williams, they are far less interesting than the present. In some of the short poems in "The Descent of Winter," he is so intent on catching the pure pigment of the present that he seems to have jotted down a note rather than worked out a poem. Yet even so brief an observation as "Between Walls" is a poem by Williams' standards, for poetry may be "the picking out of an essential detail for memory, . . . a sort of shorthand of emotional significance for later reference." [26]

In "Brilliant Sad Sun," the essential details come together to show the triumph of the present over the idealized past:

> Lee's
> Lunch
>
> Spaghetti   Oysters
> a Specialty   Clams
>
> and raw Winter's done
> to a turn — Restaurant: Spring!
> Ah, Madam, what good are your thoughts
>
> romantic but true
> beside this gaiety of the sun
> and that huge appetite?
>
> Look!
> from a glass pitcher she serves
> clear water to the white chickens.
>
> What are your memories
> beside that purity?
> The empty pitcher dangling
>
> from her grip
> her coarse voice croaks
> *Bon jor'*
>
> And Patti, on her first concert tour
> sang at your house in Mayaguez
> and your brother was there

> What beauty
> beside your sadness — and
> what sorrow (*CEP*, 324).

Williams does not reject memories entirely, for he recognizes that any poet is very much concerned with them.
He is "the watcher and surveyor of that world where the
past is always occurring contemporaneously and the present
always dead needing a miracle of resuscitation to revive
it." [27] But to make his memories as immediate as the
present, he views them with detachment.

Nevertheless, Williams is quick to banish the nostalgic.
In "Good Night," he observes himself standing in his
kitchen, filling a glass with water, when suddenly three girls
pass by the window. He yields to sentimental recollections
but only for a moment:

> it is
> memory playing the clown —
> three vague, meaningless girls
>
> . . . .
> Parsley in a glass,
> still and shining,
> brings me back. . . . (*CEP*, 145, 146)

His return is an aesthetic victory over nostalgia. What is the
romantic escape into memory worth beside this living
green? The past that his companion in the café sees is fanci-
ful and unreal; it pales before the brilliance and purity of
the present.

To show unity in what looks like disorder: this is what
Williams tries to do in his poems. In "Brilliant Sad Sun,"
the transparency of the water and the glass come together
in his sight with the white chickens — a rare moment that
flashes upon his mind, says Williams elsewhere, "from a
clean/ world" (*CEP*, 382). The same thing happens in "The
Red Wheelbarrow," with its white chickens and rainwater
glaze, and in "Nantucket," where the white curtains, the
glass tray, the glass pitcher, and the "immaculate white
bed" are one in his sight. The imagination joins things

while it preserves their perfections. But their unity is as fragile as the objects it holds together. If one of them is removed — the clear water that the woman has been pouring, for example — the scene changes character: the empty pitcher dangles and the coarse voice of the woman destroys what dazzled him there.

Williams would like to make poetry out of the most ordinary material in our lives. Quite in keeping with this desire, "Brilliant Sad Sun" opens with snatches from a menu. In an early poem called "Della Primavera Trasportata Al Morale" (*CEP*, 57–64), he includes not only a menu but signs of all sorts, including a pictorial label for poison and two arrows indicating "Woman's Ward" and "Private." The technique works far better in "Brilliant Sad Sun," because Williams has made an effort to blend them into the language of the poem. The menu is linked to the rest of the opening stanza with "and raw Winter's done/ to a turn — Restaurant: Spring!" and the sun seems to devour the scene with an enormous appetite. Similarly, Williams uses conversation to present a scene rather than to describe it. The greeting of the woman with the glass pitcher, for example, tells us with great economy that, although the café is American, it is run by a French immigrant, just as the penultimate stanza suggests a whole series of memories by means of a single example.

Woman, pitcher, chickens, and sunlight are so dazzling that they extinguish the weak light of remembered events. But the sun is both brilliant and sad, for it reveals both the woman pouring water to her chickens and the dissolution of that scene, as well as the sadness of the poet's companion remembering her past. Williams celebrates what is both constant and crumbling. His flowers and red wheelbarrows and old women are bound to perish. But in the poem they are universal and therefore imperishable, and the poet saves them again and again. "Poetry is a rival government always in opposition to its cruder replicas." [28] It is, says Williams, a government made of particulars, like the poem itself:

wasps,
a gentian — something
immediate, open

scissors, a lady's
eyes — waking
centrifugal, centripetal (*CLP*, 33).

chapter 3
the common life with a star:
francis ponge

The root of all that dazzles us is in our hearts.[1]

The first poet was Adam. For him, naming was knowing. In the state of grace that held the inhabitants of the garden, the name was enough to renew the union of man and thing. This union is a mark of grace; the thing waits for man to give it expression, and man does so by naming it. From that utterance arises perfect communication between man and all that is not man.

But out of grace man lives by broken knowledge. Outside the eternal present of the garden, he remembers his own death. Encumbered with his past and afraid of his future, he loses his authority. The name awakens nothing.

A poet who undertakes to restore this power of naming things is Francis Ponge. He sees the world divided into two camps: ideas and things. In the first camp he places man, together with his thoughts and feelings about his own experience. On the other side he places things. In the rift between the two, Ponge sees his task: to know concrete things as immediately as they know themselves, and to rejoice in his own existence, as if he were considering his memories of himself for the first time. For in order to know things, he must forget all that he learned about them and come like a stranger to "the silent world" (*le monde muet*).

Ponge views the history of man as the history of his imprisonment in ideas. New values gradually turn into laws, guaranteed to keep man in the center of the universe and reduce it to a field of human action. Because he would rather master things than know them, he uses things but does not take the trouble to understand them. The civilization he has evolved is really a pseudo-civilization, for it is built on only a fraction of human nature — the practical side.

Ponge wants to find a way of existing that will engage the whole man. It will work only when it is realized in action; it will perish the moment it becomes a thesis. It will deal with individuals in a world of particular things, for this is the common ground that brings men together. It will rejoice in mystery, and it will create the possibility of a human order far more vital than any social order based on a dead legacy of values. The new poetry, says Ponge, must not preserve values but destroy them.

Ponge's experience tells him that all ideas are relative to the men who hold them. Debates do not move him; he sees both sides. Poets and philosophers have invented hundreds of arguments to justify human existence; Ponge rejects them all. The poem is "a monument, a rock, in the measure which it *opposes itself* to thoughts and to the mind." [2] Ideas are to him less stable than the world he can see and touch. Things are beautiful because he does not and could not invent them. He can only discover them.

The loss of absolute values does not plunge him into despair. Ponge knows that to say the world is absurd means only that it cannot be mapped by human reason. The real triumph of reason is to recognize this. The new man Ponge hopes to create through his writing will be able without terror to see his future as something limited by the things of this world. Living among them, he will find only joy.

Camus points out that the task Ponge sets for himself is the epitome of the absurd. To find *le mot juste* is to seek an absolute in a world where everything is relative to the man who utters it. The wish to reconcile man and things, says Camus, reflects a nostalgia for the Word that brings everything together and illuminates all relationships. Ponge does not find it absurd, for he believes such an illumination is possible. He starts with a pine tree, a stone, a shell, the sun. "If I give myself over to such a subject, it is because it makes me play . . . ," he says, and "makes me finally blossom again, like a new love." [8]

Ponge believes that to speak for particular things, you must come to them in ignorance. You must approach them with no ideas about what they are or what their value is. Standing on the banks of the Seine, he lets himself know nothing save that the mud of this river is different from man and that man will become different from what he is only when he can devote himself "less to contemplating his own images than considering, once, honestly, *the mud*." [4]

Ponge's descriptions show how anything may become strange to you when you see it as something apart from you, whether it be a pine forest or a man lighting a cigarette. You can even lose the sense of your own body if you can forget the relationships between its parts. Rilke has a curious example of this in *The Notebooks of Malte Laurids Brigge (Die Aufzeichnungen des Malte Laurids Brigge)*. Malte reaches for a crayon under the table and suddenly loses the sense of his hand:

> above all I recognized my own outspread hand moving down there all alone, a little like an aquatic animal, examining the ground. I watched it, as I remember still, almost with curiosity; it seemed as if it knew things I had never taught it, groping down there so independently, with movements I had never noticed in it before.[5]

Rilke writes of the sheer terror that comes to a man who discovers that he cannot understand houses, faces, hands, and trees. For Ponge, however, the loss of meaning is the beginning of joy. Nothing is more amusing to him than the constant revolt of things against the images we impose on them. From the revolt begins the poem.

Only when Ponge stands outside the human uses of things does he find that he can truly surrender himself to their world. Their strangeness is both their tragedy and their mystery. In *The Prejudice Toward Things (Le Parti pris des choses*) or "The Sun of the Abyss" (*Le Soleil placé en abîme*) or *The Notebook of the Pine Grove* (*Le Carnet du bois de pins*), Ponge presses beyond the masks things hold up to him into the silent world itself. To take the side of things, he believes that you must first become ignorant. But Ponge is patient; he wants only to save things from our ideas about them and to return them to mystery. Before you can see the thing as it sees itself, he says, it must become strange to you.

Entering the life of a thing, says Ponge, will give you an absolute knowledge of it. This is not an absurd desire, but an experience which carries its own authority. Bergson describes it this way:

> When I speak of an absolute movement, it means that I attribute to the mobile [object] an inner being and, as it were, states of soul; it also means that I am in harmony with these states and enter into them by an effort of imagination. . . . And what I feel will depend neither on the point of view I adopt toward the object, since I am in the object itself, nor on the symbols by which I translate it, since I have renounced all translation in order to possess the original. In short, the movement will not be grasped from without and, as it were, from where I am, but from within, inside it, in what it is in itself. I shall have hold of an absolute. [6]

Ponge sees himself as the ambassador of the silent world. He believes that you can receive another existence only through the transparency of your own. You do not choose your subject; the subject chooses you, and with the opening of its heart heals the gap between man and the Other. You are a spectator, ignorant of the future, not the actor who makes the future. For Ponge, the future is unimportant. The revelation that the thing offers him initiates him into eternity. "These returns of joy, these renewals in the memory of objects of sensation, here are precisely what I call the reasons for living," says Ponge. "If I call them reasons, it is because they are returns of the mind to things. It is the mind alone that renews things." [7]

But knowing is more than an experience; it is making. The experience renews Ponge's creative power, but it does not relieve him of his task of making, in Wallace Stevens' words, "fictions that result from feeling." "It is the *mundo* of the imagination in which the imaginative man delights and not the gaunt world of the reason," writes Stevens. "The pleasure is the pleasure of powers that create a truth that cannot be arrived at by reason alone, a truth that the poet recognizes by sensation." [8] This statement could be taken as a defense of all Ponge's work. The poet creates an *other* nature that shows you the one that sleeps under your senses.

Ponge wants to remake the world because he believes that nothing has been properly expressed. Knowing begins with naming, and the act of naming should renew your contact with the thing.[9] But in ordinary language, the name not only fails to do this; it actually conceals things. Ordinary language maintains the stereotypes that come from not seeing the particular thing but rather the use you want to make of it. When Ponge says "replace the name," he does not mean replace it with a definition. Definitions fail because they leave out what makes a thing unique, just as descriptions fail because they are arbitrary and always incomplete. He wants a verbal equivalent different from either of these: a "description-definition" falling somewhere in between the two. He is no specialist. When he defines the object, he returns it to common experience. When he describes it, he enumerates nothing, because the thing is more than a collection of characteristics. The verbal equivalent must have an order and complexity equal to that of the original.

But in shaping the knowledge he brings back from the silent world, Ponge is faced with the possibility of distorting it. The verbal equivalent must depart from the natural object to show how the mind has kindled it, yet it must also resemble it. Standing before the Seine, Ponge asks himself how he can make a text equivalent to the river. The unity of his subject cannot be set down intact; it must be un-

rolled in time. How, then, shall he begin? With the sky and
the clouds? the weather? the swimmers?

But still, how to give an account of the depth of the
waters? And the bed of ooze or the stones on which
they roll, how to prepare it for them? And the grasses,
the rushes, the reeds that the water stirs, that it combs
as it passes, confusedly, passionately?

. . . .

How to pass to the interior of the central text, allegedly
showing the letters of the liquid material, or how to
bring to the surface that which swims or floats at the
interior or on the top of the waters? The infallible
cruising of the fish, the crucifix or the horizontal wheel
embedded in soft material, or the indolent intra-uterine
capers of some drowned man, traveling in the fetal position? [10]

Ponge gets around these problems with a highly flexible
genre, which he calls a poem, a prose poem, or a verbal
equivalent. He is not interested in the technical distinctions
between prose and poetry. Although he calls himself both a
poet and an artist in prose, most of his pieces are written in
prose. He defines the poem as an object of joy proposed for
man. It works if it expresses the particular perfections of
whatever he is writing about. These determine the form, for
like any organic creature, the poem forms itself according to
its own laws. If a poem gives you the joy that comes from a
renewed contact with your world, then it satisfies Ponge's
requirements.

Nothing makes Ponge's ideas about things clearer than
the poems themselves. I will look at three short ones, "The
Oyster" (L'Huître), "Snails" (Escargots), and "Notes for a
Sea Shell" (Notes pour un coquillage), because they treat a
similar subject in three different ways. In "The Oyster,"
Ponge sets out to show the life of things by addressing himself to the other camp: the man who abuses things.

The oyster, the size of an average pebble, is of a
rougher appearance, a less even colour, brilliantly whit-

ish. It is an obstinately closed world. Yet it can be
opened: then you must hold it in the hollow of a cloth,
use a jagged equivocating knife, try several times. Curious fingers cut themselves at this, break their nails: it
is rough work. The blows you give it mark its envelope
with white circles, with kinds of halo.[11]

Ponge starts with a comparison that places the thing in
its own world. He is not given to making statements about
things, since he prefers to show them in action, but when he
does, he gives you facts, not his personal feelings. The oyster, he says, is an obstinately closed world, yet it can be
forced open by the curious. It resists those who pry the
shell; yet to those who approach it another way it might
open of its own will. Ponge does not suggest another way,
for those who understand the failure of force do not need to
be told. And so the oyster, with the white marks of finger-
nails and knife blows left like halos on the shell, becomes a
kind of martyr. Yet once opened it does, after a fashion,
show you its treasures:

Inside you find a whole world, to drink and eat: beneath a *firmament* (properly speaking) of mother-of-
pearl, the heavens above collapse on the heavens beneath to form no more than a pool, a slimy greenish
bag, which flows and ebbs in smell and sight, fringed
with a blackish lace along the edges.[12]

The two halves of the shell, like the firmament, divide
the waters above and below it, before they are gathered together into one place to let the land appear. But here there
is no gathering of the waters and no shaping of continents.
The heavens above collapse on the heavens beneath to form
only an amorphous pool, flowing and ebbing to smell and
sight. The man who pried open the shell hoped for more.
Yet Ponge shows him only what he is capable of seeing: a
whole world to drink and eat, a world at the service of man.
"Sometimes, very rarely, a pearl formula in their mother-of-
pearl throat, from which you can at once find a means of
adornment." [13] Ponge does not approve of this. If the heav-

ens are empty and show you no more than a slimy greenish pool, you have looked for the wrong thing and missed the revelation that can only be granted by the creature itself.

In "Snails" (*Escargots*), Ponge writes for a different audience: not the man who dominates things, but the man who learns from them and would find himself at home in Aesop's universe. Like "The Oyster" (*L'Huître*), this poem opens with a statement of what the snail is not: "Unlike cinders, which are the inmates of hot ashes, snails love the damp earth." [14] Ponge justifies these dissimilarities by playing on the sound of the words *escarbilles* (cinders) and *escargots* (snails). But more important, he tries to make you forget your habitual response: "slow as a snail."

Ponge shows you the snail's life, not with adjectives, but with verbs. The snail does many things, of course, but a list of all its activities would not make you understand snailness. He asks, what is it like to live at the bottom of a shell? For the shell is the very skin of its life, inseparable from the animal inside it. Ponge tries to answer from the snail's point of view:

> Certainly it is sometimes an inconvenience to carry this shell everywhere with them, but they don't complain about it and finally they are content. It is valuable, wherever they may find themselves, to be able to retreat into themselves and defy intrusions. That is well worth the pain.
> They slobber with pride at this faculty, at this convenience. How can it be that I am so sensitive and so vulnerable a being, and at the same time such a shelter against the assaults of the troublesome, possessing such happiness and tranquillity. From hence comes this marvelous bearing? [15]

He roots the snail's consciousness in the material world. The glistening silver secretion the snail leaves in its wake is its pride. The secretion is not a symbol for pride; it *is* pride. This merging of matter and feeling lets Ponge create a moral universe without straying from the testimony of his senses. "Is the anger of snails perceptible?" he asks. If he could adjust his eyes to the smallest nuances of its life, surely it would be. "Since it is without gesture, doubtless it manifests itself only through a secretion of slime . . . ," he suggests. "One sees that the expression of their anger is the same as that of their pride." [16]

The inner life translated into the outer one is a creature's expression of itself. Of the snail's expression, Ponge observes that its secretion becomes brilliant on drying and vanishes with the next rain. The snail does not try to express itself in a more permanent form. The traces it prints as it moves across the world will vanish forever when it dies. This is all the expression it desires. Snails, therefore, belong with heroes and saints rather than with artists. The artist's work stands outside his life; the saint's work is his life. The snail's shell that allows him to retreat from the world is the foundation of his being, well worth the pain it costs him to keep it. It is a snail's tangible monument to the unfolding of its life. But the saint leaves no shell behind him. What sort of monument does his life construct? Ponge replies that the saint expresses himself in the secretion peculiar to man: the word.

When Ponge speaks of man's life, he seems to be standing among things, looking across them back at man:

The great thoughts come from the heart. Perfect yourself morally and you will make beautiful verses. Ethics and rhetoric are joined in the ambition and the desire of the wise man.

But snails are saints in this respect: they obey precisely their nature. Therefore, first of all, know yourself. And accept yourself as you are. In accordance with your vices. In proportion with your limits.

But what is the notion proper to man: the word and ethics. Humanism.[17]

By taking the side of things, Ponge reveals a way of discovering values that never lose their flexibility, because they cannot be cut loose from experience. Like things, they are always in the process of being born for you. "The poet never proposes a thought but an object," says Ponge; "that is to say, even with a thought he must cause it to take the stance of an object." [18] In doing so, Ponge establishes poetry as the place where truth is destroyed before it turns into law. Like a creature lifted from the sea, truth loses its brilliance whenever you abstract it from experience.

"Notes for a Sea Shell" *(Notes pour un coquillage)* accomplishes the same change of perspective from the world of man to that of things, with this difference: You do not see the life of the object but the poet writing the poem. It is a direct statement of Ponge's ideas about art, and they arise from his close scrutiny of a material thing. I call them ideas, but they have the solidity of things, for they cannot stand apart from the things that express them.

Ponge begins by turning his eye into a microscope. "A seashell is a small thing, but I can measure it by putting it back where I found it, placed on the stretch of sand." [19] Now, to measure here is not quantitative but qualitative; the poet measures the value of life, which is invaluable. When he pays attention to the grains of sand running through his fingers, they become important, and when the object becomes important, says Ponge, it is no longer small. And now when he examines the shell, it is as vast and precious as the temple of Angkor or the Pyramids.

Ponge loves the shell because it has the shape of the life that inhabited it. Looking at the shell, you see the animal, its limits and its fragility. And if you are Ponge, you admire how truthfully it shows you your own life. For to recognize your limits is to see yourself as you are: a physical thing that will change and die. For all these reasons Ponge loves the shell: "We are with it right in the flesh, we do not leave nature: the shell-fish or crustacean are there present." [20]

When Ponge tries to see Rome or the Pyramids as a perfect expression of the species that created them, he cannot find anything in them that tells him about man. "Man's monuments resemble the pieces of his skeleton or of any skeleton, great fleshless bones," Ponge writes; "they invoke no inhabitant of their shape." Such monuments glorify no one. "When the master leaves his dwelling," Ponge continues, "he certainly makes less impression than when the hermit crab lets his monstrous claw be seen at the mouth of the magnificent horn that shelters him." [21]

In the disparity between our lives and our monuments Ponge sees the view we have of our own importance in nature, a view he recognizes but does not share. "I am not denatured to the point of breaking with my species," he explains, "nor mad to the point of considering man as anything other than a mite." [22] The great sin against nature is to believe oneself immortal. The cathedrals, the coliseums, the Pyramids were born of this sin, of our desire to conquer time by leaving monuments that will endure forever. Ponge feels that the work of art not only should respect our limits but should rejoice in them. If man, too, made a shell no larger than his body, it would reflect his genius for adjustment, not for disproportion. Ponge himself admires art that shows the depth and variety of the finite — the music of Bach and Rameau rather than Beethoven, the poems of Malherbe, Horace, and Mallarmé, rather than Hugo and Shelley.

Above all artists, Ponge admires the writers because their medium is uniquely man's:

> their monument is made from the true common secretion of the shell-fish man, from the thing the most proportionate and conditioned to his body, and yet the most different from its form that can be imagined: I mean the WORD. [23]

He identifies the shell with the word because both are processes of nature. Ponge accepts no promises of immortality. He has too much respect for the things of this world.

> O Louvre of books, that may be inhabited after the end of our race perhaps by other guests, some monkeys, for instance, or some bird, or some superior being, as the crustacean takes the place of the shell-fish in the bastard tiara.
>
> And then, after the end of the whole animal kingdom, the air and sand in little grains slowly enter it,

> while on the ground it still shines and wears away, and
> will disintegrate in brilliance, O sterile, immaterial dust,
> O shining remnant, though endlessly turned over and
> ground between the rollers of air and sea, AT LAST!
> *Someone* is no longer there and can form nothing again
> from the sand, not even glass, and IT IS FINISHED! [24]

He sees his poems as acts of faith, which ask you to rejoice in the perishable and eternal present. It is perishable,
because everything in our lives passes. It is eternal, unbroken
by fear of the past or future, as long as you live in harmony
with this world which you know you will lose.

In "The Sun of the Abyss" (*Le Soleil placé en abîme*)
Ponge makes a verbal equivalent on the grand scale; it is
nearly thirty-four pages long. But the problems of defining
and describing his subject have not changed.

> What is the sun as object? — it is the most brilliant
> object in the world.
>
> YES, brilliant to such a degree! We've just seen how.
>
> It needs a whole orchestra to express it: the drums,
> the bugles, the fifes, the tubas. And the tambourines,
> and the drum roll.
>
> All this to say what? — A single monosyllable. A
> single onomatopoetic monosyllable.
>
> The sun cannot be replaced by any logical formula,
> because the sun is not an object.
>
> THE MOST BRILLIANT object in the world is
> not — because of this — NO — *is not* an object; it is a
> hole, it is the metaphysical abyss: the formal and indis-
> pensable condition of everything in the world.
>
> . . . .
>
> Why isn't the sun an object? Because it creates and
> kills, indefinitely re-creates and kills the subjects that
> regard it as an object. [25]

To remake the sun in words, Ponge creates a new genre of
writing: the *objeu* (thing-game). He begins with a profusion
of ambiguous and apparently arbitrary materials, and so
many viewpoints that it is impossible to choose between
them.

The *objeu* is like a jewel of which the facets are paragraphs. Each new paragraph is haunted by the earlier ones, and the whole work moves forward through a juxtaposition of themes and through successive approximations that unite all possibilities of a thing's excellence.[26] The titles of the sections into which "The Sun of the Abyss" (*Le Soleil placé en abîme*) is divided will give an idea of how various the possibilities are: "The Sun's Spinning Top" (*Le Soleil toupie a fouetter*), "The Sun Read Over the Radio" (*Le Soleil lu a la radio*), "The Fastigiate Sun Flower" (*Le Soleil fleur fastigée*), "Seals of the Sun" (*Scelles par le soleil*), "The Sun Titles Nature" (*Le Soleil titre la nature*), "The Baroque Night" (*La Nuit baroque*), "The Sun Rising Over Literature" (*Le Soleil se levant sur la littérature*). "The Sun's Spinning Top" (*Le Soleil toupie a fouetter*) is repeated twice, like a refrain. Ponge does not want us to forget that the sun is always a top to spin, a thing for man to play with and rejoice in if his mind will set it into motion.

The method of "The Sun of the Abyss" links Ponge closely with Wallace Stevens. In "Thirteen Ways of Looking at a Blackbird" or "Sea Surface Full of Clouds," Stevens also tries to show the rich possibilities of a thing's existence. Both men share a faith in the power of metaphor, the supreme fiction that gives us back the freshness of the world and the freshness of ourselves. Ponge's writings about the sun are supreme fictions that lift it from the gaunt world of reason to the world of the imagination. But Ponge extends Stevens' method to include not only the varied repetition of images, but different kinds of writing as well — poems, myths, etymological speculations, ranging in style from the sparse to the surrealistic.

Ponge's metaphors turn the sun into a kind of Proteus. The cold fires of science were never so joyful: "Dazzling sea-urchin. Woolen ball. Cog wheel. Punch in the face. Life-preserver. Club. . . . Yolk, wheel and cascade; sheaf and pump. . . . a tyrant and an artist, an artificer, an actor! Nero! Ahenobarbus!" [27] His longer descriptions are cosmogonies that are difficult only if you try to explicate them, for Ponge does not take man as his point of reference. Everything is possible here, as in a dream, but not our dream; the sun's:

> The head of the immobile lion of the sun is opposed (but it challenges, nevertheless) to the galloping herd of giraffes, the fearful and fierce flock of flames.
> A jaw strives for only one thing: its prize.
> The fixed eye of the sun is opposed to the active and bloody jaw of the flames.
> The billiard ball, the eye enshrined in the forehead of the sky. . . .
> The thimble of the sun pushes into all the senses a thousand piercing and painful needles, which effect a kind of bleeding.
> The egg of the sun gives birth to the aviary of flames. And reciprocally, the cocks of flames, at the climax of their intensity, give birth to the egg of the sun.[28]

To see things in a manner acceptable to them, Ponge says, you must remember your common denominator, death. And so he creates fables to make you feel a kinship that has led many writers into despair. Imagine that the sun has expelled some of its opponents and exiled them to a certain distance so that it may be contemplated by them. They are far enough away to cool but not to escape its attraction, and they cannot leave the orbit that obliges them to serve as witnesses of its glory. Imagine that their cooling is the slow fulfillment of the death sentence which accompanies all created things into

> this malady, . . . this tepidity that we call life. . . . Dream how much nearer to death our life is, this tepidity, than to the sun and its millions of degrees centigrade!
> I would say as much for forms and colors, which express the particular damnation of each being, of each spectator exiled from the sun. Its damnation, that is to say, its particular fashion of worshiping and dying.[29]

Ponge's ideas come across as physical processes, and his views have the irrefutability of concrete things. You can disagree with ideas, but you cannot disagree with trees and stones. And because Ponge never makes things conform to ideas, the most ordinary occurrences — rain falling, shadows lengthening — take on the quality of parables. Of the great casks of the sky, he writes that the sun is the radiant stopper, covered with a dust rag of clouds.

> When the stopper gives way, and the wave (pure and dangerous) gushes out, that is what Goethe saw at the hour of his death as he described it to us: "More light." Yes, perhaps this is what it means *to die*.[30]

He cannot show the light without showing darkness, for man feels his dependence on the sun most acutely when it is absent. The sun's ascent and journey into decline is the journey of our lives. "Rapidly then the shadow gains the text, which soon ceases to be readable," writes Ponge. "It is then that the nocturnal *outcry* resounds." [31] The shadow, the sign of your own death, is always present in moments of joy:

> The Sun, its hands open: prodigal magnificent grandfather. Sower. . . . With his warm caress, this prodigal old man abuses his descendants, hastens the course of their lives, exalts, then physically decays their bodies. . . . Each thing wears a shield, divided into silver and black.
>
> In sadness, in gloom (grey weather, cloudy, sunless), you find more equality in life.
>
> The shadow always has a form, that of the body which casts it.
>
> It is the prison (mobile), the geometric zone of punishment (involuntary) in one region of space by another's joy (or glory).
>
> Finally, it is as gloomy as joy is intense (dazzling).
>
> But this punishment is ephemeral, or at least changeable, capricious. "Each in its turn," you might say. And this is what makes it bearable.
>
> In short, at the very instant the sun strikes something with joy, it obliges it to assume responsibility, and each thing then condemns — and executes judgment, punishment.

The sun, which slaps its face with joy, at the same time dresses each thing in its judge's black robe.[32]

The shadow not only falls between the poet and things whose lives he wants to enter, it also divides him from himself: he can never forget his own death. His own life becomes a commodity to be held onto. "This divorce between man and his life, the actor and his setting, is properly the feeling of absurdity," writes Camus.

If I were a tree among trees, a cat among animals, this life would have a meaning, or rather this problem would not arise, for I should belong to this world. I should *be* this world to which I am now opposed by my whole consciousness and my whole insistence upon familiarity. . . . And what constitutes the basis of that conflict, of that break between the world and my mind, but the awareness of it? [33]

The parable of the shadow raises the question, how can you live without despair when even in ecstasy you must wear the colors of your death? Some choose to passionately accept the lack of order and affirm an unintelligible universe. "Cold (and sharp) gloom is the only thing that can make me assent to the sun." [34] Worse than living without the sun is living with the progressive ice in the sunless air of a cave. But if you know your life serves no special purpose in the general scheme of things, you will no longer trouble yourself about a creator of whose workings you know nothing. The coming of night relieves you of your duty to praise the sun by showing you the stars. The sun is only another star, in an infinity of stars. "The nearest and most tyrannic, certainly. But finally, just one of the stars." [35]

The universe of the man who lives through the agony of this view is like a cosmic artillery, supported by the horror our globe inspires in itself as well as the sun. Why shouldn't the sun, appalled at man's pride and egoism, offer its light in explosions of disgust? Ponge suggests the word *repulsion* here for its association with pyroballistics.

But then he looks at the motions of the universe in another way: "It is an artillery which, suddenly charmed, has turned into clockwork. An artillery in which the bullets have become wheels. . . ." How does anger suddenly turn to harmony and artillery to clockwork? How does violence suddenly give place to "the harmonious functioning and the silence, or rather, to the murmuring, the humming of the whole game?" [36]

The harmony that Ponge finds in the world begins with the harmony that he finds in himself. It begins with acceptance and ends with a desire to be wholly what you are, obeying all the limitations of your nature. This means, of course, that you no longer wish to be God. Living in accordance with your nature, you find your desires changed. The divorce between man and his life comes from the divorce between man and things; whether he can renew contact depends on how he chooses to know things. "Why isn't the sun an object? Because it is that which . . . kills . . . the subjects that regard it as an object." [37] The sun is no object but a living presence that the poem brings into the game. The poet has no choice but to remake the sun. You are healed when you know how to praise:

> To begin the hymn again voluntarily. To give assent to the sun in good faith. This, too, is in the power of language. To be pleased with it, to rejoice. To celebrate it. To honor it, to sing it, trying only to *renew* the themes (and variations) of this song of degrees.
>
> . . . .
>
> It is necessary to "remake" it meta-logically, to possess it.
> With great joy.
>
> . . . .
>
> To change evil into good. The forced labor in Paradise.
> Then to end in ambiguity, disdainful, ironic and tonic all at the same time: the verbal function with neither a laudative nor a pejorative motive: the objeu. [38]

It is not only the sun that kills when we make it an object; Ponge believes that man too must be renewed and celebrated, and our lives are never in great danger than when this is forgotten. The earthly paradise is not the past and it is not the future; it is now. You cannot expel the hangman from paradise, but you can walk in step with time and find in this harmony "the respite, . . . the vacation of the hangman. The common life with a star. . . ." [39]

how to live:
rainer maria rilke

> Oh, tell us, poet, what do you do?
> > — I praise.
> But those dark, deadly, devastating ways,
> how do you bear them, suffer them?
> > — I praise.
> And then the Nameless, beyond guess or gaze,
> how can you call it, conjure it?
> > — I praise.
> And whence your right, in every kind of maze,
> in every mask, to remain true?
> > — I praise.
> And that the mildest and the wildest ways
> know you like star and storm?
> > — Because I praise.[1]

A work of art, says Rilke, is the product of having been in danger, of having gone to the very end of an experience, beyond which no man can go further. It should spring from necessity, and be judged by its origins, that is, by the dangers that had to be overcome. For the danger is as necessary as the suffering it brings.

> Art, as I conceive it, is a movement contrary to nature. . . . If the meaning of sacrifice is that the moment of greatest danger coincides with that when one is saved, then certainly nothing resembles sacrifice more than this terrible will to Art. . . . All that the rest for-

get in order to make their life possible, we are always
bent on discovering, on magnifying even. . . . Unless
one assigns to the act of victory a mysterious and far
deeper meaning, it is not for us to consider ourselves
the tamers of our internal lions. But suddenly we feel
ourselves walking beside them, as in a Triumph, without being able to remember the exact moment when
this inconceivable reconciliation took place (bridge
barely curved that connects the terrible with the
tender . . .) .[2]

*The Notebooks of Malte Laurids Brigge (Die Aufzeich-
nungen des Malte Laurids Brigge)* is a record of the terrible
before it meets the tender, and Rilke warns that it must be
read against its current, for it is not directed against life but
against human weakness and error. The power that feeds
Malte's suffering could also nourish his joy. Rilke calls the
book a negative mold of which the grooves are suffering,
though the casting would be bliss.

Two of the greatest contradictions that Malte faces are
God and death. Rilke blames Christianity for nearly extin-
guishing God in human experience. A God held by belief
or the forcing of the heart to hold something as true leads
to a distinction between the saved and the damned that has
no basis in human experience. "The view that one is sinful
and needs ransom as premise for God is more and more repugnant to a heart that has comprehended the earth."[3]
Such a view leads you to condemn suffering, and to suppress
impulses in yourself which, although sometimes called evil,
may hold your real strength.

Confronted by the suffering of a whole city, Malte in
Paris feels himself annihilated. The sick and the dying
evoke his sympathy so strongly that he is left dissolved,
without will, desire, or defence, like a vacant spot. He walks
behind an epileptic on the street, and he feels his own
strength pass into the body of the sick man. Rilke is Malte
here. "I was torn out of myself . . . through all their bur-
dened lives," he writes from Paris to Lou Andreas-Salomé.
"I often had to say aloud to myself that I was not one of

them, that I would go away again from that horrible city in which they will die." [4] Malte prays that God will grant him the grace to write beautiful verses and thus prove to himself "that I am not inferior to those I scorn." [5] He pities them but he cannot accept their suffering.

Neither can he accept his own. Every fear he has ever pushed aside now returns to plague him, like a disease that has been superficially treated and breaks out in a more terrible form than before. His own "lions intérieurs" lead him through an abyss that he can only interpret as a fall from grace. Yet he knows that the saved find God in the abyss as well as in the light. The abyss holds the possibility of his salvation, just as in the myths where dragons turn into princesses; our inner dragons, says Rilke, delay transformation only to see us brave. Like the saint in "The Temptation" (Die Versuchung), Malte cannot drive his devils away without losing his angels as well. Because dividing experience into good and evil leads to spiritual impoverishment, Rilke redefines religion: "In the infinite extent of the universe it is a direction of the heart." [6]

Christianity promises to take away the fear of death. In practice, it denies death altogether and substitutes for it the belief in a Beyond. "Does death really become less opaque because these lighting devices have been dragged into place behind it?" Rilke asks.[7] Through the deaths that occur in The Notebooks of Malte Laurids Brigge and Malte's attitude toward them, Rilke tries to show that people no longer understand what death means. It remains the great contradiction, the opponent of life, the frail glass of our happiness, out of which we may be spilled at any moment.

Rilke rejects a Beyond because it denies this world for the sake of one unknown to us. As a result, the dead and our whole past are inaccessible to us. Malte clings to the absolute power of time, which his experience constantly denies. This power orders most people's experience; things happen within their appointed boundaries, and events are fairly predictable. When he loses faith in this order, he loses the sense of both his past and his future. The character of

Count Brahe suggests another way of looking at time. In his consciousness, all awareness of change has disappeared. Chronological sequence means nothing and neither does death, since for him everyone he has ever taken into his memory continues to exist. But Malte, denying his past and thereby losing his future, is left with no more room to stand on than a tin soldier. Having eliminated what he cannot understand, he becomes one of the disinherited children of the seventh *Duino Elegy* (*Die siebente Elegie*), "to whom no longer what's been, and not yet what's coming, belongs." [8]

If you reject what you cannot understand, you will find that life is indeed simpler for you, but, at the same time, more uncertain. You cannot be sure of your progress, because you cannot distinguish between problems actually solved and problems only postponed. So your life unfolds like a desert, for nothing can take root there. When a tree grows, death grows there as well as life, says Rilke; because it is full of death, it sends out a rich expression of life. So the man who is learning how to live must bring back God and death as a necessary part of human experience.

Rilke believes that you see things as they are only when you can affirm the unity of all existence, a unity in which suffering, death, and the unreality of the past are no longer a threat. Only then can you see that terror and bliss are two faces of a single head that looks in one direction or another, depending on how you meet it. Malte himself knows this, without being able to act on it. He says, "If my fear were not so great, I should console myself with the fact that it is not impossible to see everything differently and yet to live." [9] Although he is afraid to change, he admits that he feels himself standing before something magnificent. One more step and he could understand and approve of his suffering; his misery would be bliss. But he cannot take that step and he feels that he is broken.

To keep from being broken you must be as strong as water; beat it and it yields, yet it is still water. So a man, too, can choose to be changed instead of broken by suffering. "These states of rigidity may easily be transformations, inner alterations, to be followed by renewed existence and awareness of ourselves when the alteration has taken place." [10] Malte prays that he might not be inferior to those he despises. But grace can come to him only when he includes them in his prayer, when he does not see what is repulsive, but what is.

An artist who sees things as they are does not select from the world; he transforms it. Nothing so terrifies him that he cannot make it into something that affirms existence. Rilke's favorite example of this phenomenon is Baudelaire's "A Carcass" (*Une Charogne*), but in a poem to Baudelaire he praises all artists who have been able to create out of their own suffering.

> Only the poet has re-integrated
> the world that in each self disintegrates.
> The strangest beauty he's authenticated,
> even what tortured him he's celebrated,
> and ruin so infinitely expurgated
> that norm appears in what annihilates.[11]

When you can affirm even your terrors, they show you a different face. "*Death* is the *side of life* averted from us, unshone upon by us," says Rilke. Our lives belong to both realms, they are nourished by both: "*there is neither a here nor a beyond, but the great unity.*" [12] Here you cannot tell if you are moving among the living or the dead, for your existence is so broad that everything is possible in it. And this, Rilke believes, is what is required of us: to hold fast to what is difficult and love even the abyss. The laws which created the abyss are beyond human insight. We must not be deceived by events that shape the surface of our lives, for in the depths all becomes law.

Rilke calls these depths "the open" (*das Offene*) and describes it in this way:

Extensive as the "external" is, it scarcely bears comparison, for all its sidereal distances, with the dimensions, *with the depth dimensions of our inner being*, which does not even need the spaciousness of the universe to be in itself almost immeasurable. . . . It appears to me more and more as if our customary consciousness inhabited the apex of a pyramid whose base in us (and in a sense beneath us) spreads to such breadth that, the farther we find ourselves capable of letting ourselves down in it, the more generally do we appear to be included in the given facts, not dependent on time and space, of terrestrial, of, in the broadest sense, *worldly* existence. Since my earliest youth I have entertained the conjecture (and have also, as far as I sufficed, lived by it) that at some deeper cross-section of this pyramid of consciousness mere *being* could become an event for us, that inviolable presentness and simultaneity of all that which, at the upper "normal" apex of self-consciousness, it is granted us to experience as mere "sequence." [13]

This is the open consciousness of the nonhuman world, which Rilke describes so well in the eighth *Duino Elegy* (*Die achte Elegie*). The animal lives in eternity, unaware of its own death:

> Where we see Future, it sees Everything,
> itself in Everything, for ever healed.[14]

Time has collapsed into space, into an incessantly created present. But this space is like none we have ever known:

> *One* space spreads through all creatures equally —
> inner-world-space. Birds quietly flying go
> flying through us. Oh, I that want to grow,
> the tree I look outside at grows in me! [15]

Here is the place where personal experiences become impersonal, which they must be before they can be made into art. This process, as Rilke sees it, has three parts: first, you gather experiences (*Erlebnis*); then you forget them, and they become part of all that has happened to you (*Erfahrung*); and finally, called back by insight or accident, they return, impersonal and anonymous. At first you are

"The Stranger" (*Der Fremde*); you collect impressions of people and places which you do not possess:

> knowing more deeply one could never bide;
> then, already round the next curve speeding,
> other highways, bridges, landscapes, leading
> on to cities darkness magnified.

> And to let all this, without all craving,
> slip behind him meant beyond compare
> more to him than pleasure, goods, or fame.[16]

In *The Notebooks of Malte Laurids Brigge* (*Die Aufzeich-nungen des Malte Laurids Brigge*), Rilke suggests the breadth of knowledge that a poet must have. For the sake of one verse he must have known the sick, the dying, the be-loved, the movements of animals, the gestures of flowers, the screams of women in childbed, and many roads in many countries. He should wait and gather experience before sit-ting down to write. But, more important, he should not write of these things too soon. He must forget them and have the patience to wait until they come again. Not till then can the poem happen. For verses are not merely feel-ings; they are experiences (*Erfahrungen*). Although Rilke seems very close to Wordsworth here, he avoids Words-worth's word, "recollecting":

> Recalling won't suffice here, from those moments
> there must remain a layer of pure existence
> upon my being's floor, a sediment
> of measurelessly overflowing solution.
> For I'm not *recollecting* — all I *am*
> bestirs me now because of you.[17]

You can decide to recollect your past, but you cannot make it transform itself and return, innocent as a landscape, and wholly alien to you. You cannot will your experiences to the level of artistic estrangement. Rilke has this transforma-tion in mind when he says that art starts from an anony-mous center.

But the poet is more than an aeolian harp who merely responds to winds from the depths of his own consciousness. Rodin's maxim, "toujours travailler," which Rilke was fond of repeating, means that the artist can transform the whole of his experience into art. Like the *Handwerker*, he should be capable of continuous creation. It is most important, says Rilke, not to remain with the intention, but to convert mood and intention into things. He once remarked that in a successful poem of his there was more reality than he could ever find in his relationships with people: "Where I create, I am true, and I would like to find the strength to base my life entirely on this truth . . . that is sometimes given to me." [18]

Of his life in Paris, from which Malte's story grew, Rilke remarked that he would have been spared much suffering if he had been able to objectify his fears, to shape things from them, and so set himself free by the very act of creation. For when the painting has been painted or the poem written for others to read, then your experience ceases to be a part of you. From that time on, the bridge between the artist and what has happened to him is broken. The experience is as objective, says Rilke, as a Cézanne object, which is his way of describing the detachment implicit in the rendering of it. The work of art is the knot in the rosary where your life utters a prayer; it renews, over and over, the anonymous center of your existence. Whatever the artist's stated intention may be, his real purpose is to reach what Rilke calls a more intact state in the center of his own being.

The artists who do this most easily are those who have a tangible medium of presentation for all things, regardless of subject matter. Rodin could see the particular world as a system of surfaces; his medium shaped what he saw. Rilke, too, wished to be a craftsman. He was not interested in a sculptural reshaping of his work, however, but in the inward shaping of artistic processes. He knew that what he needed most was clay rather than an instrument of feeling, a medium through which he could shape the whole of his life.

But for a poet, where does this medium lie? In a more thorough knowledge of his own language and its past development? In a particular study or cultural background? Rilke's attempts at study programs always broke down, due to the strange feeling that he was returning by a round-about way to some inborn knowledge, and he soon admitted that the poet's medium is not any intellectual pursuit. Lou Andreas-Salomé had warned him that words do not build like stones. Because they are symbols for indirectly transmitted suggestions, they are far less substantial than stones. To create, the poet must learn how to live.

Four poems, taken together, show the development of Rilke's ideas on this: "The Spanish Trilogy" (*Die Spanische Trilogie*), "The Bowl of Roses" (*Die Rosenschale*), "Turning" (*Wendung*), and Sonnet 4, Part I, of the Orpheus collection (*Die Sonette an Orpheus*). "The Spanish Trilogy" is a sort of narrative of the creative process, as Rilke sees it. The poet asks that he may be able to keep the detachment that he needs if he is to turn the events of his life into art:

> Out of that cloud, look, that so wildly hides
> the star that peered this instant — (and myself),
> out of that mountain-land beyond, possessing
> night and her winds awhile now — (and myself),
> out of this river in the vale, that catches
> the gleam of torn sky-clearings — (and myself);
> out of myself, Lord, and all that, to make
> one single thing: myself here, and the feeling
> with which the flock, penned in the fold, endure
> the great dark no-more-being of the world
> with sighing breath, — myself, and every light
> in the dim multitude of houses, Lord,
> to make a thing; from strangers (for, indeed,
> I don't know one of them), and from myself,

myself, to make one thing: from all those sleepers,
those strangers, those old men up at the hospice,
coughing importantly in bed, those children,
heavy with slumber, at such strangers' breasts;
from much that's vague, and always from myself,
myself alone and all I do not know,
to make the thing, Lord, Lord, Lord, Lord, the thing,
that, cosmic-earthly, like a meteor
comprises in its weight only the sum
of its own flight, weighing only its arrival.[19]

In the first stanza, he gathers experiences, or rather impressions, most of them fleeting and remote. The star looks out of the cloud for only an instant, the gleam in the river is about to disappear, the children, the sleepers, and the old men, seen from a distance, remain strangers to him. Whether the poet is the Stranger (*Der Fremde*), or Malte, or Rilke, his view of things is that of a traveler, sensitive to beauty that goes unnoticed by those who live in its midst. Ignorance and solitude shape his vision, for he sees the repetition of everyday lives as something unfamiliar, lit by the depths of his own world.

But gathering experience is not enough; art comes "from much that's vague, and always from myself" (*aus vielen Ungenaun und immer mir*), and the repetition of "und mir" after each group of concrete details shows how important a role "myself" has. The self here is, of course, the impersonal self. When your attention is most turned outward, says Rilke, all the impressions you have collected achieve themselves without your conscious effort. Then the most accidental event will be enough to make them return and bring the inward and the outward vision together in a single moment. This finding of oneself again (*Sich-wieder-finden*) is like a comet whose significance to the viewer is its arrival. The business of making a poem, as Rilke describes it here, starts with the unexpected coming together of your own remote and varied experiences.

But the past returns only if the poet is ready, and he

can receive it only if he is free from interruptions and distractions.

> Oh, why must someone always be assuming
> such load of alien things, like a poor porter,
> heaving a more and more remotely filled
> basket from stall to stall, and stumbling after
> one whom he can't ask: Master, what's the feast for?
>
> Oh, why must someone stand here like a shepherd,
> exposed to such excess of influence,
> with such a share in this place full of happening,
> that, if he. merely leant against a tree-trunk
> in the landscape, he'd fulfill his destiny?
> And yet his too large vision be denied
> the quiet flock's appeasement, and each glance,
> above, below, be full of world, world, world?
> What gladly cleaves to others penetrating
> as blindly and inhospitably as music
> into his blood, to change there and pass on.
>
> He'll rise up night by night and have the call
> of birds outside already deep within him;
> feel bold, to be receiving all those stars
> into his gaze, not lightly — not like one
> spreading this feast of night before a woman,
> and spoiling her with all the heavens he's felt.[20]

Although the artist must protect himself for the sake of
his inner peace, he is also committed to accepting all experience. Unless he is ready for everything, he is not really
alive. Whoever questions this is like the porter, forced to
take on burdens whose purpose he cannot understand,
though he knows they are the preparations for an unknown
celebration. The master who has imposed these spiritual
burdens on him is, in Rilke's world, the angel who exists in
das Offene. Names do not count here, and personal memories have disappeared: "One must arrive there as one arrives
among the dead, surrendering all one's strength into the
hands of the Angel that is leading one." [21]

Rilke's oblique description of this consciousness in lines six through ten becomes clearer when it is read with his short essay, "An Experience" (*Erlebnis*). There he tells how, leaning against a tree in a state of nearly unconscious contemplation, he became aware of faint vibrations passing from the heart of the tree into his body. It seemed to him that his body was being treated like a soul and that he was able to receive an influence imperceptible to him under ordinary physical conditions. The spiritual distance from which he saw things gave them an inexhaustible significance and gave him a knowledge of them so complete that it seemed to come from a mutual transparency; the call of a bird outside was within him.

This experience never let him forget the cleavage in ordinary consciousness between man and what is outside of him. We never have pure space before us, says Rilke in the eighth *Duino Elegy* (*Die achte Elegie*); for us there is always World "and never nowhere without no." [22] To be human is to be always self-conscious about being alive. The "quiet flock's appeasement" (*stille Milderung der Herde*) describes more than the innocence of the animals. In the first poem of the trilogy, Rilke names, but does not define, "the great dark no-more-being of the world" that the penned-up flock endures (*das große dunkle Nichtmehrsein der Welt*). Metaphysical doubts do not shake the peace of an animal, since no self-consciousness divides it from itself. This is the peace that the poet needs if he is to take things into his feeling. Unlike the poet who celebrates his own feelings toward what he sees, the objective poet lives in two worlds at once, the inner and the outer. Only in this way can he change the events of his life into the impersonal reality of art.

The last poem resolves the problems raised in the earlier stanzas:

Let me, though, having once more the thronging of towns
and tangled skein of sounds and chaos
of vehicles round me, uncompanioned, —

let me, above the enveloping whirl,
remember sky and that earthy brim of the vale
where the homeward-faring flock emerged from beyond.
Let me feel stony, and let
the shepherd's daily task seem possible to me,
as he moves about and tans and with measuring stone-throw
mends the hem of his flock where it grows ragged.
His slow but laborious walk, his pensive body,
his glorious standing-still! Even to-day a god
might secretly enter that form and not be diminished.
Alternately lingering and moving like day itself,
while shadows of clouds
pass through him, as space were slowly
thinking thoughts for him.

Let him be for you what he may. Like a fluttering nightlight
into a mantling lamp, I place myself within him.
A light grows peaceful. Death
may cleanlier find his way.[23]

The poet prays for the shepherd's stony resistance to distractions. He is like Rodin, "blunt and hard toward the unimportant, and he stands among people as though surrounded by old bark," says Rilke. "But . . . he is wholly open when he is among things or where animals and people touch him quietly and like things."[24] The shepherd appears again in a short poem which Rilke wrote in 1926:

> They must be stationed like a shepherd, keeping
> his lonely watch: one might suppose him weeping,
> till, coming close, one feels his piercing sight;
> and, as for him the speech of stars is clear,
> for them must be as intimately near
> what climbs in still procession through the night.[25]

The poet keeps watch as well, and, like the shepherd, he feels the things of this world pass through him undisturbed. His transparency allows him both to gather experience and to affirm it. For the sake of his work, he surrenders himself to "the great dark no-more-being of the world" (*das große dunkle Nichtmehrsein der Welt*), and comes at last to know death itself, not as destruction but as change.

In "The Bowl of Roses" (*Die Rosenschale*), written some years before "The Spanish Trilogy" (*Die Spanische Trilogie*), Rilke makes, in language, a single object: a bowl of roses. This poem differs from the others in the *New Poems* (*Neue Gedichte*) in that he tries to show not only the roses but also the poet making the poem, hunting for the right metaphors to express them. Rilke starts by contrasting the roar and hurry of the human world with the space inhabited by the roses:

> Living in silence, endless opening out,
> space being used, but without space being taken
> from that space which the things around diminish;
> absence of outline, like untinted groundwork
> and mere Within; so much so strangely tender
> and self-illumined — to the very verge: —
> where do we know of anything like this? [26]

The distinction between inward and outward space is an important one here. The bowl of roses is a physical thing and occupies space. In most of the poems in the *New Poems* about flowers, animals, and things, Rilke wants only to show the qualities of their light and movement, their gestures and colors; he extends the sensual world but does not depart from it. But in the third stanza of "The Bowl of Roses," Rilke introduces another kind of space. The flowers live in an inner world of consciousness where you can no longer speak of them as separate existences. In *das Offene*, the roses are bound together by feeling at the impersonal level of consciousness.

The fourth stanza makes the distinction between physical space and inner space ambiguous. Rilke turns to the part of a rose he especially likes; the space in its heart and the complex arrangement of petals around the space, like eyelids, all of them closed,

as though they had to slumber
ten-fold to quench some inward power of vision.
And this, above all: that through all these petals
light has to penetrate. From thousand heavens
they slowly filter out that drop of darkness
within whose fiery glow the mazy bundle
of stamens stirs itself and reaches upwards.[27]

The opening of these petals to the light is like Proust's
moment of truth, when the taste of a *madeline* lights the
forgotten rooms of childhood. He had to forget the rooms
to have them return, vivid but impersonal. Forgotten, they
pass into a sleep which snuffs out the inner vision as well as
the outer, so that they are lost both to your senses and to
your memory. This sleep, as Rilke describes it, exists in no
one's mind; it is a dreamless world, the sleep without a
sleeper that he praised in his own epitaph:

> *Rose, oh the pure contradiction, delight*
> *of being no one's sleep under so many*
> *lids.*[28]

The *Weltinnenraum* ("inner world space") is not simply a
metaphor but a world of feeling with an objective existence
apart from the poet's mind. It knits everything into a single
fabric, poems with roses and roses with stars:

> And then the movement in the roses, look:
> gestures deflected through such tiny angles,
> they'd all remain invisible unless
> their rays ran streaming out into the cosmos.[29]

But in stanzas five and six, Rilke goes back to the physical flowers and describes them in a series of elaborate similes. Those in the fourth stanza are all human, as if Rilke
wants to endow the flowers with the consciousness he senses
in all things. The roses are related to one another in a small
drama that the poet seems to have overheard. Instead of
new consciousness, however, you have the pathetic fallacy.
See, he says, how

> that blusher there, as in confusion,
> has turned towards a cooler bloom, and how
> the cool one is unfeelingly withdrawing;
> and how the cold one stands, wrapped in herself,
> among those open roses doffing all.[30]

The next group of similes deals with touch and sight. One rose is like the rich color of yellow fruit, another is like a dress just flung off and still warm from human contact, a third looks like a porcelain cup full of butterflies.

But the description fails to bring the flowers to life, for no single pattern sustains the images. They are decorative rather than essential. Rilke is more interested in the roses that grow in the inner world of consciousness than in the physical flowers. For all their affinities with fruit, lilacs, dresses, butterflies, and porcelain, he knows that in the end they are like nothing else, for they contain nothing but themselves. Self-containment does not mean simply that they are closed. It means that they, like the poet himself, respond to the most fleeting events and are changed:

> to take the world
> and wind and rain and patience of the spring-time
> and guilt and restlessness and muffled fate
> and sombreness of evening earth and even
> the melting, fleeing, forming of the clouds
> and the vague influence of distant stars,
> and change it to a handful of Within?

It now lies heedless in those open roses.[31]

The roses tell him how to live, how to take the visible world into himself and change it, through feeling, into invisibility, or pure being. To be self-containing is to be like the shepherd of "The Spanish Trilogy" (*Die Spanische Trilogie*), knowing what to exclude from your attention. For Rilke, perhaps unfortunately, this means all the complex human relationships that break into his solitude and consume his strength. "That is what we have to learn," says

Rilke, "to *not* pay attention to certain things; to be *too* collected to touch them with some sensitive side when one can never come close to them with one's whole being." [32]

The poem is diffuse because Rilke wavers between the physical flowers and the inner ones, taking neither as his subject, although in this poem, the soul of the roses interests him more than their flesh. You have only to compare it with "Blue Hydrangea" (*Blaue Hortensie*) or "Persian Heliotrope" (*Persisches Heliotrop*), where he stresses the physical in all its nuances to see how the object of his poetry has changed from particular things to the spiritual world that unifies them.

In "Turning" (*Wendung*) Rilke looks at this change. The poem is a clear statement of his belief that to write from your experience, you must do more than put down what you have seen and felt. You must put all these images to sleep.

> *The way from intensity to greatness*
> *leads through sacrifice.*
> > *Kassner.*

Long he'd outwrung it with gazing.
Stars collapsed on their knees
under that wrestlerish uplook.
Or he would kneelingly gaze
and his instancy's perfume
tired an immortal until
it smiled at him out of its sleep.

He gazed at towers so hard,
he filled them with terror:
building them up again, suddenly, all in a moment.
And yet how often the day-
over-laden landscape
sank to rest in his calm perception at evening!

Animals trustfully entered
his open glance as they pastured,
and the imprisoned lions

stared as into incomprehensible freedom.
Birds flew straight through him,
kindly soul. Flowers
gazed back into him
large as to children.

And report that a *seer* was there
stirred those less,
more doubtfully, visible
creatures, women.

Gazing, since when?
How long fervently fasting,
with glance that at bottom besought?

When, waiting, he lived in foreign lands; the inn's
distracted, alienated room
morosely around him; within the avoided mirror
once more the room,
and then, from his harrowing bed,
the room again: —
airy councils were held,
inapprehensible councils,
about his still, through the painfully cumbered body,
still perceptible heart:
councils unoverheard
judged that it had not love.

(Further consecrations withheld.)

For gazing, look, has a limit.
And the on-gazeder world
wants to mature in love.

Work of sight is achieved,
now for some heart-work
on all those images, prisoned within you; for you
overcame them, but do not know them as yet.
Behold, O man within, the maiden within you! —
creature wrung from a thousand natures, creature
only outwrung, but never,
as yet, belov'd.[33]

The poet of "Turning" (*Wendung*) is no longer the traveler who collects impressions of cities, hospitals, old men, children and stars. He is the *seer*, who has learned to live like a shepherd. When he kneels in the first stanza, he becomes a thing among things, an animal who calls himself man. For whoever kneels loses the ordinary measure of his surroundings and, looking up, cannot tell what is great and what is small. But although he is now no taller than a child, he is not insignificant. "With him the scale is shifted," says Rilke, "for . . . he already belongs to that world in which height is — depth." [34]

By kneeling, the poet lets himself down into the depth-dimensions of the pyramid of consciousness. This awareness of sequence disappears: time becomes space. The freedom that makes the captive lions stare is his freedom from the prison of himself. He is the country where they are at home. He is the invisible man, not just an observer but a seer, who sees them as they see themselves. To the birds he is the very air they fly in. Rilke calls him a magician who casts a spell on *das Offene*, hoping at best to create a balance between the two of them. By resaying the names of things in the new dimension of open consciousness, he gives them expression.

But if the bond between the poet and *das Offene* is a delicate balance of powers, then in "Turning" (*Wendung*) the balance has been upset. Here he wrings the secrets from things rather than awakens them. Therefore, the towers are afraid of him, the gods grow weary under his gaze, and the stars collapse on their knees. In his strenuous observation of the concrete world, he is a craftsman who manipulates creatures and not the Orphic singer who enters their lives. Rilke sometimes regretted the *Handwerker* in himself. " 'Working after Nature' has in such a high degree made that which *is* into a *task* for me," he writes, "that only very rarely now, as by mistake, does a thing speak to me, granting and giving without demanding that I reproduce it equivalently and significantly in myself." [35]

In the *New Poems* (*Neue Gedichte*), Rilke achieved his

"Werk des Gesichts," learning from Rodin and Cézanne the patient observation of physical things. Visiting the museums and parks in Paris, listing subjects for poems, and systematically crossing out those that he completed, he sustained for a little while the ability to write without waiting for inspiration, to transform his observations — indeed his whole life — into art. He soon realized that this kind of transformation made dazzling poems but did not really open the secret lives of things: "I sit here and gaze and gaze until my eyes hurt, and . . . recite it to myself, as though I were supposed to learn it by heart, and still haven't got it." [36]

The turning in the poem, then, is from a superficial mastery of things to a real one, which comes only when he loves what his sight has gathered. On the first draft of the poem, Rilke makes this clear: *May this gazing out of myself, which consumes me to emptiness, be got rid of through a loving preoccupation with interior fullness.* [37] Once he wrung their natures from them; now he loves them as part of his own life. The "inneres Mädchen" has no counterpart in the external world, but is made of a thousand natures that have slept in him and created her. To love means to change things "entirely, within our invisible hearts,/into — oh, endlessly — into ourselves!" [38]

The *Sonnets to Orpheus* (*Die Sonette an Orpheus*) are hymns to this change that keeps things rather than kills them. Now, when Rilke writes of a rose, he no longer encumbers it with elaborate metaphors; he speaks directly to the flower of the inner world:

> For centuries your fragrance has been calling
> its sweetest names across to us;
> suddenly it lies in the air like fame. [39]

The horse in Sonnet 20, Part II, is not placed in a luminous void like so many of Rilke's animals in the *New Poems* (*Neue Gedichte*). It is as close to him as his own breath, safe from the changes that destroyed the horse he saw. "What is

time? — *When* is present? Across so many years he sprang,
with his utter happiness, into my wide-open feeling." [40] The
young girl made of a thousand natures, the horse he had
forgotten, the rose that grows in space and out of time, all
come back to him in an unbroken present. "How nothing is
ever lost!" [41]

The fourth sonnet in Part I shows how both Rilke's
method and his object have changed:

O you tender ones, step now and then
into the breath that takes no heed of you;
let it part as it touches your cheeks,
it will quiver behind you, united again.

O you who are blessed, o you who are whole,
you who seem the beginning of hearts.
Bows for the arrows and targets of arrows,
tear-stained your smile shines more everlasting.

Fear not suffering; the heaviness,
give it back to the weight of the earth;
the mountains are heavy, heavy the oceans.

Even the trees you planted as children
long since grew too heavy, you could not sustain them.
Ah, but the breezes . . . ah, but the spaces . . .[42]

Now, when he writes about the woman who loves without being loved in return, he does not take the viewpoint of
an individual. Whatever singled her out has fallen away
and left the core of her feeling standing free. She is not described; there is no one to describe, just as the man who rejected her has also lost his identity. All you can know for
certain is that his coldness closes behind her love as heed-
lessly as water.

The poet asks of the woman in the sonnet only what he
asks of himself: to live so openly that she can affirm all that
happens to her, even this loss. Only then will the direction
of her feeling be endless. Then she is both the bow and the

target, self-containing and complete. The images in the poem are simple; they describe nothing, they are the language of feeling itself. The parallel structure of verses and lines gives the poem the stark simplicity of a hymn: "Bows for the arrows and targets of arrows" (*Bogen der Pfeile und Ziele von Pfeilen*), "the mountains are heavy, heavy the oceans" (*schwer sind die Berge, schwer sind die Meere*), "Ah, but the breezes . . . ah, but the spaces . . ." (*Aber die Lüfte . . . aber die Räume . . .*). Because he writes about all women, the poet names them more truthfully than history named them: "O you tender ones" (*O ihr Zärtlichen*), "O you who are blessed, o you who are whole" (*O ihr Seligen, o ihr Heilen*). Their life in the *Weltinnenraum* is what endures.

The salvation of things, then, lies in the poet, but the salvation of the poet lies in the poem. Only he can turn loss into joy when he steps into the darkness of his own mind and recognizes there all that he has ever seen or felt. Rilke learns how to live from his angel, who is blind and gazes into himself at the whole world. In order to see things as they are, the poet too has become divinely blind.

chapter 5
radiant bread for
the sun of man:
pablo neruda

> . . . I seek not shelter
> in the hollows of weeping: I show
> the stock of the bee: radiant bread
> for the sun of man . . .[1]

The poet who takes his residence on earth seriously is like the deep-sea diver: he practices his birth again and again. And each time he is born, he finds it painful to walk as a man walks, to think as a man thinks, to begin again.

> The way of the diver
> is hazardous? The vocation
> is
> infinite.[2]

Neruda's ocean is the concrete world. To most men, it is as remote as undersea treasures, because civilization means conquering things, not expressing them. Civilized man takes minerals, wood, and fruit from the earth — not to know them but to use them. Neruda is like Wallace Stevens' necessary angel; in his sight we see the earth again. We also see each other. In that sight, the earth is our common ground, not our ideas about it. So Neruda starts by asking, What is the life of man? In what part of his speech, in which of his motions do you find it? Just as man uses the things of this earth without really knowing what they are, so he kills men without asking what he kills. Neruda stakes his whole life on the answer.

> Give me for my life
> all lives,
> give me all the sorrow
> of everyone [3]

To practice your birth means that you are willing to start over. The answers you find will not look like answers at all but more like experiences. "I did not come here to solve anything," says Neruda.

> I came here to sing
> and for you to sing with me. [4]

The concrete world shows him the spectacle of its own destruction, a spectacle so common that few people notice it. Neruda, putting himself outside the circle of human purposes, sees that man's systematic destruction of things is subject to this general, slower destruction over which he has no control. Things fall apart as if at the mercy of invisible ravagers.

> Life grinds
> on the glasses and powders, wearing us threadbare,
> smashing to smithereens,
> pounding
> the forms. [5]

No order gives it direction, no explanation gives it purpose. Neruda sees things run their course like a projection of rapid photography.

The destruction would not be so appalling if it did not include man. Is it weakness and fear, asks Neruda, that make us want to endure forever? Stripped of all our metaphysics, we are no more permanent than tables and chairs. Surely we need a new language to mourn our dead. In his elegy for Alberto Rojas Jiménez, Neruda finds one. He takes man out of the fortress of his ideas and puts him back into chaos:

> Between terrified feathers, between nights
> and magnolias and telegrams,
> between southerly winds and winds from the sea blowing
>   West,
>   you come flying.
> . . . .
> Over drugstores, committees,
> over lawyers and navies, wheels
> and the reddened extraction of teeth,
>   you come flying.[6]

His anguish lights the brilliance and desolation of a world seen without eyelids. Everything in it is crumbling, and he himself is as diffused and formless as the rain. Death permeates his vision of things like an obsession:

> I see, alone, at times
> coffins with sails,
> bearing away pallid dead, women with dead tresses,
> bakers white as angels,
> pensive girls married to public notaries,
> coffins ascending the vertical river of the dead,
> the purple river,
> upstream, with sails filled by the sound of death
> filled by the silent sound of death.[7]

Suddenly it seems "all that is living concludes in my feet," says Neruda. "From there on, the hostile and alien begins." [8] Things are strange to him because he can no longer express them. When the tidy categories of noun and verb disappear, everything conspires to form a single nameless substance. Under all the names and uses we give to things, he finds there is something dense and unified lying underneath. "Things of leather, of wood, of wool, . . . unite around me like walls." [9] Sartre calls it nausea:

And then all of a sudden, there it was, clear as day: existence had suddenly unveiled itself. It had lost the harmless look of an abstract category: it was the very paste of things, this root was kneaded into existence. Or rather the root, the park gates, the bench, the sparse grass, all that had vanished: the diversity of things, their individuality, were only an appearance, a veneer. This veneer had melted, leaving soft, monstrous masses, all in disorder — naked, in a frightful, obscene nakedness.[10]

Perhaps no poem of Neruda's shows better what it means to live with such anguish than "Walking Around":

It happens I'm tired of being a man.
I enter the tailor shops and the movie houses
withered, impenetrable, like a felt swan
navigating in a water of origin and ashes.

The odor of barbershops makes me cry aloud.
I only wish a repose of stones or of wool,
I only wish not to see establishments or gardens,
or merchandise, or eyeglasses, or elevators.

It happens I grow weary of my feet and my nails
and my hair and my shadow.
It happens I'm tired of being a man.

Still, it would be delightful
to frighten a notary with a spliced lily
or lay low a nun with a jab to the ear.
It would be lovely
to walk the streets with a green knife
and scream until I die of the cold.

I don't want to go on being a root in the dark
vacillating, shivering from sleep,
reaching downward, into the wet entrails of the earth,
absorbing and thinking, eating each day.

I don't want so much misfortune for myself.
I don't want to go on as root and as tomb,

subterranean only, of a wine cellar with corpses,
stiff with cold, dying of misery.

That is why Monday flares like petroleum
when it sees me approach with my jailhouse face,
and howls on its course like a wounded wheel,
and takes steps of warm blood toward night.

And pushes me to certain corners, to certain damp houses,
to hospitals where the bones come out of the window,
to certain shoestores that smell of vinegar,
to streets terrifying like crevices.

There are birds the color of sulphur and horrible intestines
hanging from the doors of the houses I hate,
there are forgotten dentures in a coffeepot,
there are mirrors
that should have wept from shame and terror,
there are umbrellas everywhere, and poisons, and navels.

I stroll with calm, with eyes, with shoes,
with rage, with forgetfulness,
I pass, walk across offices and orthopedic shops,
and patios where clothing hangs from a wire:
drawers, towels and shirts that weep
slow dirty tears.[11]

What is man when you take away his grammar, his
purposes, his metaphysics? He is a thing among things, with
no way of keeping his identity in the plentitude of the concrete world. Neruda knows that unless he loses himself he
cannot enter the lives around him. Yet this transparency
opens him to chaos. Sounds wrinkle him and objects pass
through him. He is a phantom, a man without qualities, in-
vaded by stones, wool, elevators, gardens, and eyeglasses. Everything that strikes his senses strikes his heart. A man
grows tired of being a man when he tries to endure in a
world where nothing endures and everything buckles under
the same lawlessness.

The poem is dense with images of things that do not
"belong" together: teeth, coffeepots, umbrellas, and navels

all tumbled together as if a storm had wildly displaced
them. The things that sicken him most are those that keep
people from seeing themselves as they are: movies, barbershops, elevators, and false teeth. A man wearing false teeth
forgets the fact of his own decay. He goes to a movie to let
others live his life. The elevator makes him forget how to
walk, and the barbershop fixes his mind on the changes of
human fashion.

These things support your illusions by not letting you
grow out of them. It is easy to justify your life if you trim
away whatever threatens to change it. The notary takes his
authority from man-made laws rather than natural ones.
The nun takes hers from beliefs that praise the spirit by denying the flesh. But the sin of the tailor against the fullness
of life is a parable that includes all others. His art hides nature and persuades you to love an illusion:

Clothes have their existence: they have colors and patterns
    and forms,
and live deep — far too deep! — in our myths;
there is too much shelter and furniture loose in the world,
while the flesh lives defamed, in a welter of scurrilous
    things,
underneath, obsessed with its thralldom, in chains.[12]

You want to frighten notaries and murder nuns when you
find yourself so isolated that violent contact between people
seems preferable to none.

What Rilke writes of Malte's crisis is equally true of
Neruda's: anguish is a mold, the grooves of which are agony
and the casting joy. To cast his joy, he goes to the kingdom
of death and brings back a new way of being alive. "If we
are already dead, if we come from the deep crisis, we lose the
fear of death." [13] Instead of asking that he might keep his
identity, Neruda asks that it be changed.

Ah, may I continue being and ceasing to be,
may my obedience order in itself such iron conditions,

that the tremor of deaths and of births do not shake
the deep place which I would reserve eternally.

Let me be, then, what I am, in some part and at all times,
an established, assured and ardent witness,
carefully destroying and preserving himself without ceasing
plainly pledged to his first duty.[14]

After *Residence on Earth* (*Residencia en la tierra*),
Neruda writes a different kind of poetry. Though he prom-
ised to tell the sorrows of all men, the despair of these
poems is personal. Both his style and his subjects are remote
from common experience. But he knows his poems will not
change anything unless people can understand them. He
wants them to be as familiar as stone and wood, as necessary
as a tool for the hand. To make his poetry effective as an
instrument of social action, he simplifies his style. The im-
petus for this came with the Spanish Civil War, which
showed him a struggle more urgent than his own: the
steady erosion of the oppressed by the oppressor.

The *Canto General* (*General Song*), a long collection of
poems published in 1950, makes good and evil real again.
Its divisions outline the action of a drama: *The Lamp in
the Earth* (*La lampara en la tierra*), *The Liberators* (*Los
liberatores*), *The Betrayed Arena* (*La arena traicionada*), *The Earth Is Called John* (*La tierra se llama Juan*), *I
Am* (*Yo soy*). On one side Neruda sees the earth, the animals, the rivers, and the men who live close to these things.
On the other side he sees the conqueror who sins against nature by appropriating the lives of others. From the meeting
of the conqueror and the conquered emerges the liberator
who gives back, over and over, the justification for a man's
life to the man who lives it.

An odor stayed on in the cane fields:
carrion, blood, and a nausea
of harrowing petals.
Between coconut palms lay the graves, a stilled
strangulation, a festering surfeit of bones.

A finical satrap conversed
with wineglasses, collars, and piping.
In the palace, all flashed like a clock-dial,
precipitate laughter in gloves, a moment
spanning the passageways, meeting
the newly killed voices and the buried blue mouths.
   Out of sight,
lament was perpetual and fell, like a plant and its pollen,
forcing a lightless increase in the blinded, big leaves.
And bludgeon by bludgeon, on the terrible waters,
scale over scale in the bog,
the snout filled with silence and slime
and vendetta was born.[15]

The relation between the oppressed and the oppressor unfolds through a series of actions. Each image centers around an active verb: stayed (*ha quedado*), converses (*conversa*), flashes (*brilla*), falls (*cae*). They are facets of a single process, set down by a man who has detached himself so that he can see all sides. The difference between the bitter invective of "The Dead in the Square" (*Los muertos de la plaza*) or "To Miguel Hernandez" (*A Miguel Hernandez, asesinado en los presidios de España*) and the cold brilliance of "The Dictators" (*Los dictadores*), "The Beggars" (*Los mendigos*), or "Hunger in the South" (*Hambre en el sur*), is the difference that Ezra Pound saw between William Carlos Williams and himself. "Where I see scoundrels and vandals, he sees a spectacle or an ineluctable process of nature." [16] In his best writing, Neruda follows Williams' advice: to maintain the force of his assault, he stands remote from the field. "His senses remain unclouded so that ours too may remain unclouded — as our hearts are wrung." [17]

Neruda fails as a witness when he identifies good and evil with political systems alone, that is, when he cuts his tale to fit his ideas. In the long paeans to Stalin and Molotov in "Let the Rail Splitter Awake" (*Que despierte el leñador*), Neruda has forgotten what he himself believes: that man cannot be saved by ideas but only by the acts of other men. For evil does not start with systems but with the men who make them.

When the poet turns executioner, he loses the wholeness of vision which lets him see clearly. He is the judge who demands punishment without mercy.

> I do not want to shake hands all around and forget;
> I do not want to touch their blood-stained hands;
> I want punishment.[18]

At the beginning of World War I Rilke, too, wanted punishment and even wrote several patriotic hymns. He later rejected them and took a more detached position: surely somewhere in space someone could see this suffering as one of the rhythmic convulsions of the universe, even when everything that he loved was going under. Neruda, like Rilke, writes best when he wants to heal, not to destroy. As a political fugitive in Chile, he saw the loyalty and the suffering of his people firsthand. Their wasteland hangs on no myths and no symbols. It is a real place with real names. Good and evil are local circumstances. When Neruda asks, "What is man," he does not hear the pages of history turning, but something else:

> And I heard a voice welling up
> from the dense base of the pyramid
> as if the womb of hell had cried aloud,
> and there lurched forth a creature with no face,
> a foetus like a mask all splattered over
> with sweat and blood and dirt.
>
> And that nameless thing cried to me, saying, "Wherever
> you go, tell of the torment endured
> by those on the bottom, O my brother,
> tell of your brother, whose whole life
> is lived on the rim of hell."[19]

Neruda writes out of love and a readiness to love. Speaking against the atom bomb to the people of North America, he rejoices in the physical acts that bind us to-

gether and to the earth: walking, eating, sleeping, making
love. For he cannot speak and be heard unless his hearers
have this readiness, too:

> You are
> what I am, what I was, what we must
> protect, the fraternal sub-soil
> of pure America, the simple
> men of streets and roadways.
> My brother Juan sells shoes
> just like your brother John,
> my sister Juana peels potatoes
> just like your cousin Jane,
> and my blood is of miners and sailors
> like your blood, Peter.[20]

Neruda goes among the farmers, the sailors, the miners,
and the fishermen of his country and finds that no one has
really spoken to them or caught the idiosyncrasies of their
thought and speech. The titles of Neruda's poems about
them tell you where he stands: the earth is called John. The
simple man who lives close to the earth shall inherit it. Neruda also knows that no one is simple in the sense that he
can be taken for granted. To be simple is to follow Whitman's advice for the shaping of future poets:

> Love the earth and sun and the animals, despise
> riches, give alms to every one that asks . . . , hate
> tyrants, . . . go freely with powerful uneducated per-
> sons, and with the young, and with the mothers of
> families — re-examine all you have been told in school
> or church or in any book, and dismiss whatever insults
> your own soul; and your very flesh shall be a great
> poem.[21]

The vulnerability that destroyed Neruda in *Residence
on Earth* (*Residencia en la tierra*) is his strength in the *Elemental Odes* (*Odas elementales*). All things speak to him,
and he sings of their miseries and joys. They come to him, he
says, with the naked hue of an apple; in his poems, they

are born over and over. Neruda says little about poetic technique. Learning how to write starts with learning how to
live:

> I live,
> I love,
> and I am loved.[22]

Nothing is excluded from his love. Wheels, coal sacks, bar-
rels, and baskets lead him back to the earth. The new poetry will be as impure as our bodies, soiled by sweat and
usage and traffic with the things of this world. If you can
keep this joyful contact with things, you are already a poet,
even if you have never written a word, for being a poet
means living so selflessly that nothing is alien to your singing.

> I wish
> that all should live
> in my life
> and sing in my song,
> I have no importance,
> I have no time
> for my affairs
> by night and by day
> I must note down what happens
> and forget no one.[23]

Such a poem is a gift, the signature of his love. Neruda
recalls how as a child he discovered a hole in the hedge that
surrounded his house. As he watched the hole, a child's
hand appeared and deposited the gift of a toy lamb. Neruda responded by leaving a favorite pine cone in place of
the lamb for the unknown giver. This mysterious exchange,
he says, has remained at the bottom of his heart like a sedi-
ment, feeding and inciting his poetry. "Poetry is discovered
a step at a time, in the midst of things and beings, not by
separating them, but by bringing them all together in a
blind extension of love." [24] Neruda celebrates this love. But
he can only give to whoever is willing to receive.

> I am simply people, hidden door,
> dark bread, and when you receive me
> you receive yourself, that guest
> so many times struck down
> and so many times
> reborn.[25]

Because he wants to make peace between man and the earth, Neruda rejects all poetry written out of despair. Unable to deny his own crisis in *Residence on Earth* (*Residencia en la tierra*), he transfers the blame from himself to the political system. Explaining why he will not include his early work in a collection of his poems for Communist youth, he says, "I did not want the reflections of a system which had driven me almost to despair to deposit on the rising towers of hope the terrible slime with which our common enemies had muddied my own youth." Because Eliot and Sartre have found a wasteland in a universe of love, Neruda calls them the apostles of a great charnel-house the capitalists are preparing. "Before the monopolists drop the atom bomb and annihilate a large part of the human race in defense of their unjust economic system," he writes, "these apostles have the task of annihilating men morally." [26] But Neruda forgets that the kingdoms of agony may be internal as well as external, and wholly inaccessible to social action.

The *Elemental Odes* (*Odas elementales*) are written by a man whose selfless response to things unlocks their surfaces. Neruda writes them to praise what he loves: salt and sun, flowers and stars, eyes, energy, and people. If you need a meaning for these things, you will not be at home here. Neruda builds his residence on earth out of bread, water, cereal, and light, so that the common man may find himself at ease.

> I want . . .
> . . . .
> that all should be
> cup or tool.

> In order that all may live
> in it
> I make my house
> with clear odes.[27]

In both his *Elemental Odes* (*Odas elementales*) and his earlier poems, Neruda gives himself over to particular things. But you have only to put "From: Elephant" (*Oda al elefante*) next to "Entrance into Wood" (*Entrada a la madera*), one of the "Three Material Songs" (*Tres cantos materiales*) from *Residence on Earth*, to see how Neruda's way of seeing things has changed. In "From: Elephant," Neruda does not try to give you the inner life of his subject, as Rilke would. He is a teacher whose senses are his text. Like a teacher he begins by naming its qualities.

> Gross innocent,
> Saint Elephant,
> blessed beast
> of the perduring forests
> bulk of our palpable world
> in its counterpoise,
> mighty
> and exquisite,
> a saddlery's cosmos
> in leather,
> ivory
> packed into satins
> unmoved
> like
> the flesh of the moon,
> minimal eyes
> to observe, without being observed,
> horn
> virtuoso
> and bugling
> propinquity,
> animal
> waterspout

elate
in
its
cleanliness,
portable
engine
and telephone booth in a forest:
so
softly you go
in your swagger,
with your aging caparison
in the wrinkle and pile
of a tree's regimentals,
your pants
at your ankles,
trailing your tail-end.[28]

The purpose of Neruda's description is to make you remember what you already know as if you did not know it. Stereotypes are imbedded in the careless usage of ordinary speech. Here, however, you cannot hasten over the words without noticing them, for the short lines make each word important and break your most perfunctory glance into separate images. The short phrases and the swift piling-up of descriptive clauses suggest a method of classification; yet Neruda is less interested in similarities than in differences. His metaphors are not always simple observable comparisons. They start by making the thing unfamiliar to you and end by making it new. The elephant does not look like a telephone booth in a forest. Neither "a saddlery's cosmos in leather" (*cuero de talabartería planetaria*) nor "ivory packed into satins" (*marfil compacto, satinado*) gives a clear picture of the real elephant. But Neruda is no imagist. Seeing a thing well is not enough; he wants you to love it. To do this, he crosses the avenue of man's life into the broader life of nature. Here the elephant is more than a clown and pack bearer:

he is patriarch,
father of emerald lights,

the ancient
and innocent
sire of the universe.

All the fruits of the earth,
and the longings
of Tantalus,
the multitudinous
skin
and the ways of
the rain
have encompassed
the kingdom of
elephants;
with brine
and
with blood
they accomplished the war
of their species in silence.

The scale-bearing kind,
the lizards-turned-lion,
the fish in the mountains
and gargantuan ground sloth
succumbed
and decayed:
they
leavened the green of the bog,
a prize
for the sweltering fly
and the scarab's barbarity.
But the elephant rose
on the wreck of his fears —
almost a vegetable, a shadowy pylon
in his emerald heaven,
to suckle his young
on the sweet of the leaves, and the water
and honey of stones.[29]

The elephant rules the natural universe because he endures; his domain is time and his eternity is an eternity of exits and entrances. The animal kingdom can evolve only through a series of deaths. Death as something that destroys an identity belongs only to man. Rilke knew the anguish of this when he wrote:

> If man would only cease to invoke the cruelty in Nature to excuse his own! He forgets how infinitely innocent even the most terrible happens in Nature; she does not watch it happen — she hasn't the perspective for that; she *is* wholly in the most dreadful, even her fruitfulness is in it, her generosity — it is, if one must put it that way, nothing other than an expression of her fullness. Her consciousness consists in her completeness; because she contains *everything*, she contains the cruel too.[30]

When you stand in the universe of the elephant and ask what man is, you will not find him the conqueror of nature he believes himself to be. Looking at a soldier asleep in the jungle, Neruda sees neither friend nor enemy but the fruit of a series of deaths. Even when he is killing his enemy, the soldier carries his own death. The treacherous arena of conquered and conqueror is part of the greater arena of change:

> All will be a drop in the forests,
> all will be devoured in the earth.
> . . . .
> Everything returns to the silence crowned with feathers
> in which a remote king devours clinging vines.[31]

The innocence of the elephant is the innocence all nature has when you step outside human progress to see it. It is an Eden that needs death to continue; yet it is still Eden, because the idea of sin makes no sense here. Nature is both change and the state of grace that lets you live in the whole of life rather than in your sector of it. Like the ocean, it is always washing the dead ashore; yet it absorbs them again

so completely that Neruda asks, "Where do the griefs go?"
The light from the sea is the light he himself would like to
see by:

> bring us to see, in the end,
> the sea moving, wave upon wave,
> and flower after flower, all the earth.[32]

"Entrance into Wood" (*Entrada a la madera*) gives a
negative view of the same process. Neruda again loses himself in things, but now he is destroyed by them:

> Scarcely with my reason, with my fingers,
> with slow waters slowly inundated,
> I fall under the spell of forget-me-nots,
> of a tenacious atmosphere of mourning,
> of a forgotten decayed salt,
> of a bunch of bitter clover.

> I fall in shadow, in the midst
> of destroyed things,
> and watch spiders, and graze in forests
> of secret inconclusive wood,
> and walk among damp fibers extirpated
> from the living being of substance and silence.

> Sweet matter, O dry-winged rose,
> in my sinking I climb your petals
> with feet heavy with red fatigue,
> and in your hard cathedral I kneel
> striking my lips upon an angel.

> It is I who am before your color of world,
> before your pallid dead swords,
> before your reunited hearts,
> before your silent multitude.

> It is I before your wave of dying odors
> wrapped in autumn and resistance:
> it is I undertaking a funeral journey
> amid your yellow scars:

it is I with my laments without origin,
without nourishment, without sleep, alone,
entering darkened corridors,
reaching your mysterious substance.

I see your dried currents moving,
I see your interrupted hands growing,
I hear your oceanic vegetables
rustling with night and fury shaken,
and I feel leaves dying within,
incorporating green materials
to your forsaken immobility.

Pores, veins, circles of sweetness,
weight, silent temperature,
arrows fastened to your fallen soul,
beings asleep in your dense mouth,
dust from sweet pulp consumed,
ashes full of extinguished souls,
come unto me, to my measureless sleep,
fall into my room where night falls
and falls without pause like broken water,
and clasp me to your life, to your death,
to your subdued materials,
to your dead neutral pigeons,
and let us make fire, and silence, and sound,
and let us burn, and be quiet, and bells.[33]

What does it mean to enter into the nature of a thing? When a *haiku* master enters the heart of a thing, the distinction between subject and object disappears. He does not divorce himself from a pine tree, for example, but meets it with a wholly selfless concern, making it a tree into which the human heart has entered.[34] Ponge required a whole book, *The Notebook of the Pine Grove* (*Le Carnet du bois de pins*) to describe his entrance into wood, but of how this came about he says simply that it wants to show you its heart. When Rilke writes about a panther or a gazelle, nothing else exists. His love places it in the center of the universe. On this the *Ding*-poets agree: to enter into the life of a thing, you must forget yourself so completely that you find yourself on the other side of nature, as if you had passed through a mirror. What your eyes see and your ears hear become one with all you have ever thought or felt. "All contradictions have become unified," says Baudelaire. "Man has *surpassed* god." [35]

If self-forgetfulness is the key that unlocks things, then Neruda has failed in "Entrance into Wood" (*Entrada a la madera*). He is not the invisible man who opens his heart to things; he is the encumbered man who cannot escape his own point of view. The *thou* loses his life to love another; the *I* goes under because he is unable to let it go. "It is I before your wave of dying odors," says Neruda, beating out his presence again and again. "It is I with my laments without origin." The real subject of his poem is not the quality of wood but the quality of his own despair.

In the *Elemental Odes* (*Odas elementales*) Neruda says that things choose him to say their lives. In "Entrance into Wood," Neruda chooses things to carry his own formlessness in a universe without order. The properties that furnish the slums of his soul are dead neutral pigeons, bitter flowers, silence and bells, the corrosion of salt, and the decay of living things. They appear throughout *Residence on Earth*; for example, "Ode with a Lament" (*Oda con un lamento*), "Death Alone" (*Sólo la muerte*), "Disproceedings" (*Desespendiente*), and "Sonata and Destructions" (*Sonata y destrucciones*). "Entrance into Wood" belongs with these poems.

Later, Neruda felt that his early work was too cloistered. He was a poet writing for other poets and setting himself apart from ordinary men by rarefied emotional experiences and a style remote from the spoken word. The regular lines and stanzas he admired in the work of the early Symbolists seemed a dead language. When Neruda accused the followers of Symbolism of neglecting their responsibility to humanity, he was also accusing himself:

    what did you do
in the kingdoms of agony,
in sight of a nameless humanity
and their vexed acquiescence,
heads drowned
in the offal, the harrowed
quintessence of life trampled under? [36]

Never again, after *Residence on Earth*, does Neruda
write "laments without origin." As he turns from the nuances of his own life to the lives of others, his residence on
earth opens its doors: the man who fears becomes the man
who loves. No longer do moon, water, bread, and wine
reflect a disordered imagination and a private chaos. Instead, they are the immutable foundations of order, joining
the men who share them. Poetry is not found by separating
things but by bringing them together, in a blind extension
of love.

In "Ode to Bread" (*Oda al pan*) Neruda's love for man
shapes his love for the things that man lives with.

        Bread,
        with flour
        water
        and fire
        you rise.
        Dense and light,
        recumbent and round,
        you repeat
        the belly
        of the mother,
        equinoctial
        terrestrial
        germination.
        Bread,
        how easy
        and profound you are,
        on the white rack
        of the bakery
        your rows stretch

> like tools, plates
> or papers,
> and suddenly,
> the wave
> of life,
> the conjunction of germ
> and fire
> you grow, grow
> suddenly
> like
> waist, mouth, breasts,
> hills of the earth.[37]

Neruda wants his poem to be as simple and profound as its subject. The short lines break each thought into small units, so that your mind seems to move over it inch by inch. Because he is writing to be immediately understood, he disregards the dazzling simultaneity of sensations that his complex metaphors evoke in so many of the odes and sets them down simply, one at a time.

Neruda wants to do with bread what Stevens did with his jar in Tennessee: to place it on a hill and let its presence tame the wilderness. The comparisons in the first stanza of the poem make it clear that he celebrates bread for being itself, not for being eaten. Making bread is a birth and a growing. Its shape suggests the birth of man, its growth the rebirth of spring, an "equinoctial terrestrial germination" (*equinoccial/germinación/terrestre*). It grows like a mouth, a breast, a hill, in a universe where everything is alive. Change is the sign of its life. If you cannot change, you cannot grow, and in Neruda's eyes you are less alive than the bread or the hill.

Because bread does not happen by itself, man is as much the subject of the poem as bread. But the "I" of the earlier poems has become "we," and Neruda no longer uses things to carry his private emotions.

> O bread of each mouth,
> we

will not implore you,
men
are not
beggars
of vague gods
or obscure angels.
Of the sea and the earth
we will make bread,
we will sow wheat
on the earth and the planets,
. . . .
Bread, bread
for all the peoples
and with it what has
the form and the taste of bread:
we shall distribute
the earth,
beauty,
love.
All that
which has the taste of bread,
form of bread,
germination of flour.
Everything
is born to be shared,
to be given,
to multiply itself.[38]

In bread Neruda sees the kingdom of man. Contrary to
Christian teachings, man does live by bread alone. Beauty
and love have meaning nowhere but here. The pitiful spec-
tators he sees at religious processions tell him that institu-
tionalized religion destroys those it promises to save. The
Indians are servile and abused; the hungry parochial
schoolmasters, the nuns, and the clergy have lost touch with
the earth. They deny life because they are afraid of death.
But a salvation that asks of anyone such a denial is not for
Neruda.

I did not buy a parcel of the sky
that the priests were selling, nor did I accept the obscurities
that the metaphysician manufactured
for complacent potentates.

I wished to meet death like the poor
who had no time to study it
while they were being flailed by those who have
the sky divided and arranged.[39]

Neruda's kingdom of peace on earth is to come only
when people have learned to share the gifts of the earth. It
will come through sacrifice, for the meek cannot inherit the
earth until the conqueror has been conquered and the
treacherous arena converted into the plains of peace. If
the rich hoard bread, let no man beg or pray for it; but let
him and hungry men everywhere fight for justice:

> We will go crowned
> with grain
> conquering
> earth and bread for all,
> and then
> life too
> shall have the form of bread,
> simple and profound,
> innumerable and pure.
> All beings
> shall have a right
> to the earth and to life.
> And this shall be the bread of the future,
> bread of each mouth,
> sacred,
> consecrated,
> because it will be the product
> of the longest and hardest
> of human struggles.
>
> The terrestrial victory

has no wings:
it has bread on its shoulders
and flies bravely
freeing the earth
like a baker
carried on the wind.[40]

So bread is as holy as the wafer on Sunday, and Neruda asks no greater reward than the earth itself. Those who go crowned with thorns suffer for human causes.

Although Neruda wants you to feel the urgent life of bread, too many explicit ideas make the whole effect rather flat. Ultimately, the poem has little to do with bread and everything to do with the government of man. The apocalypse is oversimplified, as in Neruda's least successful political poems, where the line between poetry and prose disappears altogether. Compared to those in "From: Elephant" (*Oda al elefante*), the metaphors in this poem are general and the rhythms weak. Furthermore, you cannot read his promise that the simple man will conquer the earth without remembering Neruda's remarks elsewhere that no one can conquer it. Both the oppressed and the oppressor are subject to the laws of nature; here, he has already said, is the real conqueror.

The *Elemental Odes* are Neruda's hymns to being alive. But he knows that the poet of life must also be the poet of death. He has answered the question, What is man, by showing man's life as part of the bigger life of nature. But although death in nature is both a midwife and an executioner, when a man dies, that particular man does not return in any season. You cannot tell what man is until you know whether there is any way of saving that particular man without bringing in metaphysics or an afterlife.

Neruda's answer is his experience. What has happened to him cannot be refuted. In his long poem "The Heights of Macchu Picchu" (*Alturas de Macchu Picchu*), Neruda makes it clear that our most intense experience of impermanence is not death but our own isolation among the living:

How many times in the winter streets of a city, or in
an autobus or a ship at dusk, or at night, in that densest
of solitude: a party, beneath sound of shadows and bells,
in that very grotto of human pleasure, I wanted to pause
and search for the inscrutable eternal vein
that I had touched before in stone,
or in the lightning unleashed by a kiss.
. . . .
I could grasp no more than a cluster of faces,
hasty masks, like an empty ring of gold,
like scattered clothes, children of a furious autumn
that would tremble the wretched tree of frightened races.[41]

One cause of man's loneliness is that, unlike all other
creatures, he lives with the knowledge of his own death. All
his life he saves time, yet at the end of his life he has saved
nothing; his anxiety floods him with choices and desires,
but like Rilke's half-filled masks in the *Duino Elegies* (*Duineser Elegien*), he seldom fulfills his role, and he ends by
setting up barriers between himself and other lives. The
difference between the simple life and the treacherous arena
is the difference between isolation and love. Civilization is
built on the failure to love. And without love, nothing of us
survives in the imaginations of those who come after us. For
permanence is what can be continued:

Fury has shrivelled up
the sad merchandise of the dealer in human beings,
while throughout a thousand years the dew
has left its transparent letter atop the plum tree,
upon the same waiting branch, . . .[42]

Neruda points out that we, unlike things, can die two
kinds of death. The great death destroys us physically; it is
natural; it is one of the changes that sustain life. The small
death destroys us spiritually; it keeps us from being reborn;
you find it in whatever confirms men in their isolation from
one another, and then, like Neruda, it happens you are
tired of being a man. For you see that men are threshed like
corn in the granary of lost deeds and miserable events,

and the sad crumbling of their days was
a black cup from which trembling they drank.[43]

If the broken fabric of our lives is everything, then nothing
of us survives and we lose even the sense of our own conti-
nuity:

I could not love the tree in every being
shouldering its diminutive Autumn
(death of a thousand leaves),
all the false dying and resurrection
without earth, without abyss:

. . . .
I rolled over and over, dying of my own death.[44]

When Neruda visited the relics of the ancient mountain city of Macchu Picchu, he first saw it as a monument to
the permanence of nature and the impermanence of man.
Not a trace of man remains. His life has disappeared along
with his knives, cloth, "customs, frayed syllables,/masks of
blazing light." [45] But nature knows no such obliteration. To
the waterfalls, rivers, and vegetation, pressed into coal deep
in the earth, destruction is a most fruitful transformation.
Of them at least, Neruda can say, even in the shadow of the
vulture, "The dead kingdom still lives." [46]

But can you say this of man? Not if you are asking for
a physical survival, certainly. Neruda reminds us that our
identity is not our physical presence alone but other men's
response to it. Love alone rescues us from oblivion. So he
calls upon the place to give up its dead, and he will resur-
rect them through his love:

Return to me the slave that you buried.
Disgorge from the earth the hard bread
of the wretched, show me the garments
of the serf and his window.
Tell me how he slept when he lived.

. . . .

and like a bird for a thousand years prisoner
let the old heart of him who is forgotten
beat within me![47]

The lost deeds that make up the life of the "inconclu-
sive man" (*hombre inconcluso*) are now the stuff of his immortality. Neruda finds that only his own life can show him
the dead and make them present to him. Trying to love the
solitudes, the dangers, and the weaknesses of those he could
never meet joins him to their lives, and in this joining Neruda sees man's indestructible return.

I do not see the swift bird of prey,
nor the blind cycle of his talons,
I see the ancient being, the servant, the sleeper
in fields, I see a body, a thousand bodies,
one man, a thousand women, . . .
rise and be born with me, brother. . . .
I come to speak through your dead mouth. . . .
Speak through my words and my blood.[48]

If Neruda is intolerant of despair, it is because he
wants nothing to sully man's residence on earth. He knows
that each man must build his own, and that Eden can sur-
vive only where your love is stronger than your knowledge
of death. As a poet, he dedicates himself to making this
happen again and again:

I feel no loneliness at night
in the obscurity of earth.
I am people, the innumerable people.
In my voice is the clear strength
that can traverse silence
and germinate in darkness.
Death, suffering, shadows, frost,
suddenly descend on the seed.
And the people seem entombed.
But corn returns to earth.
Its red implacable hands
thrust through the silence.
From death comes our rebirth.[49]

chapter 6
legacy of the invisible man

> He is the transparence of the place in which
> He is and in his poems we find peace.[1]

For Neruda, Rilke, Williams, and Ponge, the question of
how to write is a question of how to live. With the excep-
tion of Williams, seeking to justify free verse, they have little to say about the technique of writing poetry. Throughout their work they examine, again and again, the life that
a man must lead if he wants to know what is real. Their
biographies show four very different men; it is in their
poems, letters, and essays that they agree. And it is because
of their agreement that I have brought them together here.
From their writings emerges a way of life that is like the
precepts of a wise and unknown teacher. It brings together
a residue of beliefs beside which personal circumstances
hardly matter. If poets must go to school, let them be
taught by the truth that joins these lives, a truth that lies
with things, not with the interpretations we put upon them.
Those whom I have called the *Ding*-poets start with what
they see, hear, and touch. When science reduces their testimony to formulae, they reject the materialism of science.
They resist whatever promises to order their experience for
them and to dictate its significance. "The senses witnessing
what is immediately before them in detail see a finality
which they cling to in despair, not knowing which way to
turn," Williams writes. "Thus the so-called natural or scien-
tific array becomes fixed, the walking devil of modern
life." [2]

Although all four poets stand outside of organized religion, they praise men of the church whose lives show what
they see as true holiness: the reverence for life lived in the
present. The artist must accept even the most repulsive experiences as openly as Rilke says Saint-Julien-l'Hospitalier
did, lying beside the leper and sharing his own warmth in
an unconditional embrace that takes in every creature on
earth. And Williams praises the missionary friar Père Sebastian Rasles for not separating his beliefs from his sensual
experiences: "The world is parcel of the Church so that
every leaf, every vein in every leaf, the throbbing of the
temples is of that mysterious flower." [3] From the saint these
poets learn love, and they surrender their lives to enter into
the lives of others. "The only possible way that St. Francis
could be on equal footing with the animals was through the
word of God which he preached with fervent breath of understanding," says Williams. "Nor do I think it is especially
recorded that St. Francis tried to make the sparrows Chris-
tians. When the service was over each beast returned to his
former habits." [4]

Among the *Ding*-poets, the word of God is where conversation takes place; it is a common ground of understanding among creatures of this world, which must be reached
before the "I" and the "Not I" can be reconciled. The
Ding-poets recognize that most people partition their re-
sponses into what concerns them and what does not. These
partitions imprison them. The treacherous arena of the conqueror and the conquered becomes their way of life; like
things, people are to be used. These poets save us by giving
us a knowledge of our world as indisputable and vital as
the revelations of the saints. In the kingdom of man, religion is, as Rilke says, a direction of the heart. The artist,
like the saint, shows us how to love. To love, one must
make one's self invisible.

The invisible man is Neruda's phrase, but all four
poets describe him. Rilke identifies him with the artists and
saints who absorb and reflect the life of the earth: Rodin,
Cézanne, St. Francis. For Williams he is Shakespeare and

Homer, whose personal circumstances do not affect the vivid lives they describe. Ponge speaks of the invisible man whenever he speaks of the man of the future, who understands things and rejoices in their lives. In Neruda's poem, the invisible man speaks for himself:

> Give me for my life,
> all lives,
> give me all the sorrow
> of everyone,
> I am going to transform it
> into hope.
> Give me
> all joys,
> even the most secret ones,
> because if it weren't that way,
> how are they going to be known?
> I have to tell about them,
> give me
> the struggle
> of each day
> because they are my song,
> and thus we will go together,
> side by side,
> all men:
> my song reunites them,
> the song of the invisible man
> who sings with all men.[5]

When you start from the faith that there are no ideas but in things, you enter a world of such strangeness and disorder that language itself seems utterly divorced from what it has always described. To be transparent means to have an extraordinary negative capability that lets you suspend all the ideas you live by. There is no place in your life narrow enough for contradictions to meet. "We must assume our existence as *broadly* as we in any way can," says Rilke; "everything, even the unheard-of, must be possible in it." [6]

The most difficult experience to transform is death. Accepting it as part of their faith in the physical world, Williams and Ponge do not try to justify the mortality of what they love. If you are standing on a precipice and you cast your eye on something immediate so as not to see the rest, says Ponge, you will not fall into despair.

Neruda and Rilke feel, however, that the poem of death must be written to free us from the fear of death. To write it, they return man to nature, to the total life of things from which this fear has excluded him. In nature even destruction is an expression of fullness. Rilke wants to make death once more the knowing participant in everything alive. It is the side of life turned from us; it is also, says Neruda, whatever can be reborn. Their evidence rests on their experience: Neruda's at Macchu Picchu and Rilke's at Duino, where the living and the dead gather into an undivided space, a region of the deepest consciousness, says Rilke, which, in the middle of time and interruption, is mysteriously protected.

All four poets agree that the death you should fear is the death of your heart, imprisoned in a world wholly measurable, usable, and falling away under your grasp. "All things brought under the hand of the possessor crumble to nothingness," [7] says Williams. And all things flower under the hand of the man who asks nothing but to know them as they know themselves. Things are immeasurable, ungraspable, and mysterious.

This change from useful to mysterious does not happen in the world but in man himself, whenever he stops treating the thing as an object and respects it as a presence. Gabriel Marcel has described it most accurately. When a being is granted to me as a presence, says Marcel, I cannot treat him as if he were placed before me. The relationship that arises between us surpasses my simple awareness of him. For me he exists in an immediacy beyond all imaginable mediation.[8]

To the invisible man, nothing is an object and everything is a presence: seeing is loving. The *Ding*-poets distinguish between them only because for many people such a division already exists. To the feeling world of childhood, the invisible man brings the selflessness of the adult whose experience has taught him to love the community of man. Our tragedy, says Williams, is our inability to communicate with one another, locked within ourselves as we are and unable to utter the simplest things of importance.

These poems express lives that cannot express themselves, and create the kinds of encounters that break down the bars between men. So the poem is called a blind extension of love, and an object of joy proposed for man which shows the world at one with itself. While Ponge and Rilke bring men together by leading them to *le monde muet*, the innocent kingdom where things live unaware of their own death, Williams and Neruda turn to the spoken language, believing that to the poet it can reveal a whole community's way of thought. When Neruda promises to write so that everyone can understand him, when Williams listens to the rhythms of speech where lives unexpectedly open out into other lives, they are hunting for the place where real conversation takes place — the moment of equality, of balance between a man and all that is not himself. You kneel, height becomes depth, and the treacherous arena reveals itself as the plains of peace.

> I am not superior
> to my brother
> but I smile
> because I go through the streets
> and I do not exist alone,
> life runs
> like all the rivers,
> I am the unique
> invisible man,
> there are no mysterious shadows,
> there is no darkness,
> everyone speaks to me,
> they want to tell me things,
> they speak to me of their relatives,

> their miseries
> and their joys,
> everyone passes and everyone
> tells me something.[9]

This meeting is like no other. Williams calls it a rival government always in opposition to its cruder replicas. Its authority is your experience; its laws are particular questions that have no definite answer. Neruda calls himself a tranquil man, enemy of laws, governments, and established institutions, who loves disturbed and dissatisfied people, whether they are artists or criminals. Ponge agrees: The social importance of poetry is not to preserve values but to abolish them. You must not be seduced by systems. You walk through a locked world, listening for a pulse under the dead surfaces that our lives have created. Beyond the broken testimony of your senses the sea still dazzles; you remember you have seen it before, and in that instant you discover that the pulse you listen for is your own. The innocent presences show themselves once more. The root of all that dazzles you is in your heart.

notes

notes to chapter 1.

1. "The ninth elegy," *Duino Elegies*, trans. by J. B. Leishman and Stephen Spender, 75. "Die neunte Elegie," *Sämtliche Werke*, I, 718:

> Sind wir vielleicht *hier*, um zu sagen: Haus,
> Brücke, Brunnen, Tor, Krug, Obstbaum, Fenster, —
> höchstens: Säule, Turm. . . .

2. Quoted, no source given, in Marjorie Brace, "Worshipping Solid Objects: The Pagan World of Virginia Woolf," in Kerker Quinn and Charles Shattuck, eds., *Accent Anthology*, 493–94.

3. "Toward an Impure Poetry," in *Selected Poems of Pablo Neruda*, trans. by Ben Belitt, 39. "Sobre una poesía sin pureza," *Obras completas*, 1822: Es muy conveniente, en ciertas horas del día o de la noche, observar profundamente los objetos en descanso. . . . De ellos se desprende el contacto del hombre y de la tierra como una lección para el torturado poeta lírico. . . . Así sea la poesía que buscamos, . . .

For the history of the *Dinggedichte* as a genre, see "Das Dinggedichte" by Kurt Oppert in *Deutsche Vierteljahrsschrift für Literaturwissenschaft und Geistesgeschichte*, Heft. 4.

4. "Statute of Wine," *Residence on Earth and Other Poems*, trans. by Angel Flores, 89. "Estatuto del vino," *Obras completas*, 221:

> Hablo de cosas que existen, Dios me libre
> de inventar cosas cuando estoy cantando!

5. "Against the Weather," *Selected Essays of William Carlos Williams*, 197–98.

6. My translation from "Pages bis," *Proêmes*, 177: Je n'ai pas de temps . . . à prêter à l'ontologie . . . tandis que je n'ai pas assez de temps pour scruter les objets, les refaire, en tirer qualités et jouissances. . . . Unless acknowledged, translations are mine.

7. My translation from "Tentative Orale," *Le Grand Recueil*, II, 253: Ce n'est pas l'unité que je cherche mais la variété.

8. See note 14.

9. In *Selected Essays, 1917–1932*, 7–11.

10. In "A Few Don'ts by an Imagiste," *Poetry*, I (March, 1913), 200–201.

11. *Letters of Rainer Maria Rilke, 1910–1926*, trans. by Jane Bannard Greene and M. D. Herter Norton, 390. *Briefe aus Muzot, 1921 bis 1926*, 382: Das handwerklich Hinausgestellte, . . . sei eine Bildung, . . . zu der das "Ich" nur der erste und letzte Anstoß war, die aber von da ab Ihnen gegenüber bleibt, abstammend von Ihrem Impuls, aber sofort soweit fortgeschoben auf die Ebene der künstlerischen Entfremdung, des dinglichen Alleinseins, daß Sie nur noch als ein ruhiger Beauftragter an der Vollendung dieses geheim Gegenständlichen sich beteiligt fühlen.

12. My translation from "La pratique de la littérature," *Le Grand Recueil*, II, 277: J'en aurai beaucoup plus rendu compte, si j'ai fait un texte qui ait une réalité dans le monde des textes, un peu égale à celle de la pomme dans le monde des objets. Compare Rilke on Cézanne, *Briefe aus den Jahren 1906 bis 1907*, 378.

13. "Shakespeare," in *Selected Essays*, 56.

14. My translation of "Poésie et pensée abstraite," in *Oeuvres*, I, 1337: une sorte de machine à produire l'état poétique au moyen des mots.

15. "The Simplicity of Disorder," in *Selected Essays*, 99.

16. "The Work of Gertrude Stein," *Selected Essays*, 118–19.

17. My translation from *Rainer Maria Rilke — Lou Andreas-Salomé, Briefwechsel*, 92: Worte bauen doch nicht wie Steine, tatsächlich und unmittelbar, vielmehr sind sie Zeichen für indirekt vermittelte Suggestionen, und an sich allein weit ärmer, stoffloser, als ein Stein.

18. My translation from "Tentative orale," *Le Grand Recueil*, II, 257: Il faut que les choses vous dérangent.

19. "My Creative Method," *Le Grand Recueil*, II, 20: définitions-descriptions esthétiquement et rhétoriquement adéquates.

20. *Le Carnet du bois de pins* has not been translated into English.

21. "Concerning Landscape," *Selected Works: Prose*, trans. by G. Craig Houston; "Von der Landschaft," *Insel-Almanach auf das Jahr 1933*, 44: Denn man begann die Natur erst zu begreifen, als man sie nicht mehr begriff; als man fühlte, daß sie das Andere war, das Teilnahmlose. . . .

22. William Wordsworth, "Of Poetry as Observation and Description," in *Prose Works of William Wordsworth*, II, 131.

23. My translation from "De l'eau," *Le Parti pris des choses*, 40: Elle est blanche et brillante, informe et fraîche, passive et obstinée dans son seul vice : la pesanteur, disposant de moyens exceptionnels pour satisfaire ce vice : contournant, transperçant, érodant, filtrant.

24. *Letters of Rainer Maria Rilke, 1910 bis 1926*, 256. *Briefe aus Muzot*, 17: Bist du frei? Bist du bereit, mir deine ganze Liebe zu widmen?

25. "El hombre invisible" ("The Invisible Man"), *Obras completas*, 937:
> todo el mundo me habla,
> me quieren contar cosas.

26. "The eighth elegy," *Duino Elegies*, 69. "Die achte Elegie," *Sämtliche Werke*, I, 715:
> unendlich, ungefaßt und ohne Blick
> auf seinen Zustand, rein, so wie sein Ausblick.
> Und wo wir Zukunft sehn, dort sieht es Alles
> und sich in Allem und geheilt für immer.

27. "The Mountain," *New Poems*, trans. by J. B. Leishman, 291.
"Der Berg," *Sämtliche Werke*, I, 638–39:
> Sechsunddreissig Mal und hundert Mal
> hat der Maler jenen Berg geschrieben,
> weggerissen, wieder hingetrieben
> (sechsunddreißig Mal und hundert Mal)
>
> zu dem unbegreiflichen Vulkane,
> selig, voll Versuchung, ohne Rat, —
> während der mit Umriß Angetane
> seiner Herrlichkeit nicht Einhalt tat:
>
> tausendmal aus allen Tagen tauchend,
> Nächte ohne gleichen von sich ab
> fallen lassend, alle wie zu knapp;
> jedes Bild im Augenblick verbrauchend,
> von Gestalt gesteigert zu Gestalt,
> teilnahmslos und weit und ohne Meinung —,
> um auf einmal wissend, wie Erscheinung,
> sich zu heben hinter jedem Spalt.

28. "A Beginning on the Short Story (Notes)," *Selected Essays*, 307.

29. My translation from "Tentative orale," *Le Grand Recueil*, II, 257: La vérité ce n'est pas la conclusion d'un système, la vérité c'est cela.

30. *The Autobiography of William Carlos Williams*, 356.

31. *Letters of Rainer Maria Rilke, 1910–1926*, 197. *Briefe aus den Jahren 1914 bis 1921*, 249: Ihr Bewußtsein besteht in ihrer Vollzähligkeit, weil sie *alles* enthält, enthält sie auch das Grausame. . . .

32. My translation from "El hombre invisible," *Obras completas*, 940:
> dadme todo el dolor
> de todo el mundo,
> yo voy a transformarlo
> en esperanza.

33. *Letters of Rainer Maria Rilke, 1910–1926*, 325. *Briefe aus*

Muzot, 186: Die Anschauung, sündig zu sein und des Loskaufs zu bedürfen als Voraussetzung zu Gott, widersteht immer mehr einem Herzen, das die Erde begriffen hat.

34. "Worpswede," *Selected Works: Prose*, 22. "Worpswede," *Werke: Auswahl in Zwei Bänden: Prosa*, II, 239: Das ist alle Kunst: Liebe, die sich über Rätsel ergossen hat, — und das sind alle Kunstwerke: Rätsel, umgeben, geschmückt, überschüttet von Liebe.

35. *Nausea*, trans. by Lloyd Alexander, 171. *La Nausée*, 162: Les mots s'étaient évanouis et, avec eux, la signification des choses, leurs modes d'emploi, les faibles repères que les hommes ont tracés à leur surface.

36. *Nausea*, 178. *La Nausée*, 169: Tout d'un coup ils existaient et ensuite, tout d'un coup, ils n'existaient plus : l'existence est sans mémoire; des disparus, elle ne garde rien — pas même un souvenir.

37. "My creative method," *Le Grand Recueil*, II, 19: PARTI PRIS DES CHOSES *égale* COMPTE TENU DES MOTS.

38. Ezra Pound, *Instigations of Ezra Pound, Together with an Essay on the Chinese Written Character, by Ernest Fenollosa*, 380–81.

39. "Lower Case Cummings," *Selected Essays*, 266.

40. *The Autobiography*, 362.

41. Friedrich Nietzsche, *Gesammelte Werke*, XIII, 237: Hier springen mir alles Seins Worte und Wort-Schreine auf: alles Sein will hier Wort werden, alles Werden will hier von mir reden lernen.

42. "La Dérive du sage," *Proêmes*, 68: Le Verbe est Dieu! Je suis le Verbe!

43. "The ninth elegy," *Duino Elegies*, 75. "Die neunte Elegie," *Sämtliche Werke*, I, 718:

> Bringt doch der Wanderer auch vom Hange des Bergrands
> nicht eine Hand voll Erde ins Tal, die Allen unsägliche,
> sondern
> ein erworbenes Wort, reines, den gelben und blaun
> Enzian. Sind wir vielleicht *hier*, um zu sagen: Haus,
> Brücke, Brunnen, Tor, Krug, Obstbaum, Fenster, —
> höchstens: Säule, Turm . . . aber zu *sagen*, verstehs,
> oh zu sagen *so*, wie selber die Dinge niemals
> innig meinten zu sein.

44. Sonnet 11, Part I, *Sonnets to Orpheus*, trans. by M. D. Herter Norton, 37. *Sämtliche Werke*, I, 738:

> Doch uns freue eine Weile nun
> der Figur zu glauben. Das genügt.

notes to chapter 2.

1. *Paterson*, I, 14–15. All subsequent references to this book will be given as *Paterson* in the text.

2. John Dewey, *Art As Experience*, 286.

3. "Against the Weather," *Selected Essays of William Carlos Williams*, 197–98.

4. *The Autobiography of William Carlos Williams*, 362.

5. *The Collected Earlier Poems of William Carlos Williams*, 91. All subsequent references to this book will be given as *CEP* in the text.

6. *I Wanted to Write a Poem: The Autobiography of the Works of a Poet*, 35.

7. *I Wanted to Write a Poem*, 29.

8. William Carlos Williams, "Notes from a Talk on Poetry," *Poetry*, XIV (July, 1919), 213.

9. "Prologue to Kora in Hell," *Selected Essays*, 17.

10. *I Wanted to Write a Poem*, 21.

11. *The Autobiography*, 360, 362.

12. *The Autobiography*, 362.

13. *The Autobiography*, 360.

14. *The Autobiography*, 362.

15. *The Autobiography*, 288.

16. "Against the Weather," *Selected Essays*, 198.

17. *The Selected Letters of William Carlos Williams*, 136.

18. *I Wanted to Write a Poem*, 73.

19. *I Wanted to Write a Poem*, 82.

20. "Excerpts from a Critical Sketch," *Selected Essays*, 108.

21. "How to Write," *New Directions in Prose and Poetry*, 1 (1936), 57–58.

22. *The Collected Later Poems of William Carlos Williams*, 220–29. All subsequent references to this book will be given as *CLP* in the text.

23. *The Selected Letters*, 296.

24. *The Autobiography*, 360.

25. "A Beginning on the Short Story (Notes)," *Selected Essays*, 303.

26. "Author's Introduction to *The Wedge*," *Selected Essays*, 256.

27. "Introduction to Charles Sheeler — Paintings — Drawings, Photographs," *Selected Essays*, 232.

28. "The Basis of Faith in Art," *Selected Essays*, 180.

notes to chapter 3.

1. "Le Soleil placé en abîme," *Le Grand Recueil*, III, 174: La racine de ce qui nous éblouit est dans nos cœurs. Unless acknowledged, translations are mine.

2. *La Seine*, 10: un monument, un roc, dans la mesure òu il *s'oppose* aux pensées et à l'esprit.

3. "Entretien avec Breton et Reverdy," *Le Grand Recueil*, II,

299: si je m'adonne à un tel sujet, c'est parce qu'il me fait jouer . . . , me refleurit enfin comme un nouvel amour.

4. *La Seine*, 42: moins à contempler ses propres images qu'à considérer une fois honnêtement *la boue* . . .

5. *The Notebooks of Malte Laurids Brigge*, trans. by M. D. Herter Norton, 84. *Werke; Auswahl in Zwei Banden: Prosa*, 77: ich erkannte vor allem meine eigene, ausgespreizte Hand, die sich ganz allein, ein bißchen wie ein Wassertier, da unten bewegte und den Grund untersuchte. Ich sah ihr, weiß ich noch, fast neugierig zu; es kam mir vor, als könnte sie Dinge, die ich sie nicht gelehrt hatte, wie sie da unten so eigenmächtig herumtastete mit Bewegungen, die ich nie an ihr beobachtet hatte.

See also Sartre, "L'Homme et les choses," *Situations*, I, 259.

6. Henri Bergson, *The Creative Mind: A Study in Metaphysics*, trans. by Mabelle L. Andison, 159–60.

7. "Natare piscem doces," *Proêmes*, 121:

Ces retours de la joie, ces rafraîchissements à la mémoire des objets de sensations, voilà exactement ce que j'appelle raisons de vivre.

Si je les nomme raisons c'est que ce sont des retours de l'esprit aux choses. Il n'y a que l'esprit pour rafraîchir les choses.

8. Wallace Stevens, "The Figure of the Youth as Virile Poet," *The Necessary Angel*, 57–58.

9. Jean-Paul Sartre, "L'Homme et les choses," *Situations*, I, 264.

10. *La Seine*, 32, 34:

Mais encore, la profondeur des eaux comment en rendre compte? Et le lit de vase ou de cailloux sur lequel elles roulent, comment le leur préparer? Et les herbes, les joncs, les roseaux qu'elles font bouger, qu'elles peignent plus ou moins désordonnément, passionnément au passage?

. . . .

Comment faire passer à l'intérieur du texte central, supposé présentant les caractères de la matière liquid, ou flotter a sa surface, ce qui nage ou flotte à l'intérieur ou à la surface des eaux? La croisière infaillible des poissons, le crucifix ou la roue horizontale en matière molle, ou les molles cabrioles intra-utérines de quelque noyé, voyageant dans la position du foetus?

11. "The Oyster," in *The Penguin Book of French Verse: The Twentieth Century*, trans. by Anthony Hartley, ed., Vol. IV, 246. "L'Huître," *Le Parti pris des choses*, 20: L'huître, de la grosseur d'un galet moyen, est d'une apparence plus rugueuse, d'une couleur moins unie, brillamment blanchâtre. C'est un monde opiniâtrement clos. Pourtant on peut l'ouvrir : il faut alors la

tenir au creux d'un torchon, se servir d'un couteau ébréché et peu franc, s'y reprende à plusieurs fois. Les doigts curieux s'y coupent, s'y cassent les ongles : c'est un travail grossier. Les coups qu'on lui porte marquent son enveloppe de ronds blancs, d'une sorte de halos.

12. "The Oyster," 247, 20: A l'intérieur l'on trouve tout un monde, à boire et à manger : sous un *firmament* (à proprement parler) de nacre, les cieux d'en-dessus s'affaissent sur les cieux d'en-dessous, pour ne plus former qu'une mare, un sachet visqueux et verdâtre, qui flue et reflue à l'odeur et à la vue, frangé d'une dentelle noirâtre sur les bords.

13. "The Oyster," 247, 20: Parfois très rare une formule perle à leur gosier de nacre, d'où l'on trouve aussitôt à s'orner.

14. "Escargots," *La Parti pris*, 29: Au contraire des escarbilles qui sont les hôtes des cendres chaudes, les escargots aiment la terre humide.

15. "Escargots," 30:

    Certainement c'est parfois une gêne d'emporter partout avec soi cette coquille mais ils ne s'en plaignent pas et finalement ils en sont bien contents. Il est précieux, où que l'on se trouve, de pouvoir rentrer chez soi et défier les importuns. Cela valait bien la peine.

    Ils bavent d'orgueil de cette faculté, de cette commodité. Comment se peut-il que je sois un être si sensible et si vulnérable, et à la fois si à l'abri des assauts des importuns, si possédant son bonheur et sa tranquillité. D'où ce merveilleux port de tête.

16. "Escargots," 32: La colère des escargots est-elle perceptible? . . . Comme elle est sans aucun geste, sans doute se manifeste-t-elle seulement par une sécrétion de bave. . . . L'on voit ici que l'expression de leur colère est la même que celle de leur orgueil.

17. "Escargots," 33: Les grandes pensées viennent du coeur. Perfectionne-toi moralement et tu feras de beaux vers. La morale et la rhétorique se rejoignent dans l'ambition et le désir du sage.

    Mais saints en quoi : en obéissant précisément à leur nature. Connais-toi donc d'abord toi-même. Et accepte-toi tel que tu es. En accord avec tes vices. En proportion avec ta mesure.

    Mais quelle est la notion propre de l'homme : la parole et la morale. L'humanisme.

18. "Natare piscem doces," *Proêmes*, 54: Le poète ne doit jamais proposer une pensée mais un objet, c'est-à-dire que même à la pensée il doit faire prendre une pose d'objet.

19. "Notes for a Sea Shell," *The Penguin Book of French Verse*, IV, 248. "Notes pour un coquillage," *Le Parti pris*, 55: Un coquil-

lage est une petite chose, mais je peux la démesurer en la repla-
çant où je la trouve, posée sur l'étendue du sable.

20. "Notes for a Sea Shell," 251, 57: nous sommes avec lui en
pleine chair, nous ne quittons pas la nature : le mollusque ou le
crustacé sont là présents.

21. "Notes for a Sea Shell," 250, 56: Les monuments de l'homme
ressemblent aux morceaux de son squelette ou de n'importe quel
squelette, à de grands os décharnés : ils n'évoquent aucun habi-
tant à leur taille. . . . Quand le seigneur sort de sa demeure il
fait certes moins d'impression que lorsque le bernard-l'hermite
laisse apercevoir sa monstrueuse pince à l'embouchure du superbe
cornet qui l'héberge.

22. *La Seine*, 22: Je ne suis pas dénaturé au point de me désoli-
dariser d'avec mon espèce, ni fou au point de considérer l'homme
bien autre chose qu'un ciron.

23. "Notes for a Sea Shell," IV, 253, 58: leur monument est fait
de la véritable sécrétion commune du mollusque homme, de la
chose la plus proportionnée et conditionnée à son corps, et cepen-
dant la plus différente de sa forme que l'on puisse concevoir : je
veux dire la PAROLE.

24. "Notes for a Sea Shell," 253–54, 58:

> O Louvre de lecture, qui pourra être habité, après la fin
> de la race peut-être par d'autres hôtes, quelques singes par
> exemple, ou quelque oiseau, ou quelque être supérieur,
> comme le crustacé se substitue au mollusque dans la tiare
> bâtarde.
>
> Et puis après la fin de tout le règne animal, l'air et le
> sable en petits grains lentement y pénètrent, cependant que
> sur le sol il luit encore et s'érode, et va brillamment se
> désagréger, ô stérile, immatérielle poussière, ô brillant résidu,
> quoique sans fin brassé et trituré entre les laminoirs aériens et
> marins, ENFIN! *l'on* n'est plus là et ne peut rien reformer
> du sable, même pas du verre, et C'EST FINI!

25. "Le Soleil placé en abîme," *Le Grand Recueil*, III, 161–62,
179:

> Qu'est-ce que le soleil comme objet? — C'est le plus
> brillant des objets du monde.
>
> OUI, brillant à tel point! Nous venons de le voir.
>
> Il y faut tout l'orchestre: les tambours, les clairons, les
> fifres, les tubas. Et les tambourins, et la batterie.
>
> Tout cela pour dire quoi? — Un seul monosyllabe. Une
> seule onomatopée monosyllabique.
>
> Le soleil ne peut être remplacé par aucune formule
> logique, CAR le soleil n'est pas un objet.
>
> LE PLUS BRILLANT des objets du monde n'est — de
> ce fait — NON — *n'est pas* un objet; c'est un trou, c'est l'abîme

métaphysique : la condition formelle et indispensable de tout au monde.

. . . .

Pourquoi le soleil n'est-il pas un objet? Parce que c'est lui-même qui suscite et tue, ressuscite indéfiniment et retue les sujets qui le regardent comme objet.

26. See Philippe Jaccottet, "Remarques sur 'Le soleil,'" *La Nouvelle nouvelle revue française*, IV (septembre, 1956), 396–405, for a brief discussion of structure and technique.

27. "Le Soleil placé en abîme," *Le Grand Recueil*, III, 159, 175, 162:

Oursin éblouissant. Peloton. Roue dentée. Coup de poing. Casse-tête. Massue. . . . Moyeu, roue et cascade; girande et noria. . . . un tyran et un artiste, un artificier, un acteur!

Néron! Ahenobarbus!

28. "Le Soleil placé en abîme," 171:

La tête de lion immobile du soleil s'oppose à (mais pourtant il provoque) la troupe galopante de girafes, le troupeau peureux et féroce des flammes.

. . . .

Une mâchoire épouse toujours quelque chose : sa proie.

L'œil fixe du soleil s'oppose à la mâchoire active et sanglante des flammes.

La bille, l'œil enchâssé au front du ciel. . . .

Le dé du soleil s'oppose aux ciseaux des flammes.

Le dé du soleil pousse en tous sens mille aiguilles perçantes et blessantes, qui font saigner.

L'œuf du soleil donne naissance à la volière des flammes. Et, réciproquement, les coqs des flammes, à leur moment hypnotique et de plus grande intensité, donnent naissance à l'œuf du soleil.

29. "Le Soleil placé en abîme," 163:

cette maladie, . . . cette tiédeur que l'on nomme la vie. . . . Songez combien plus proche de la mort est la vie, cette tiédeur, que du soleil et de ses milliards de degrés centigrades!

J'en dirais autant des formes et des couleurs, qui expriment la damnation particulière de chaque être, de chaque spectateur exilé du soleil. Sa damnation, c'est-à-dire sa façon particulière d'adorer et de mourir.

30. "Le Soleil placé en abîme," 159: Que la bonde cède, et que le flot (pur et dangereux) jaillisse, c'est alors ce qu'a vu Gœthe à l'heure de mourir, comme il nous l'a décrit : «Plus de lumière.» Oui, voilà peut-être *mourir*.

31. "Le Soleil placé en abîme," 181:

Rapidement alors l'ombre gagne le texte, qui cesse bien-tôt d'être lisible.

C'est alors que le *tollé* nocturne retentit.

32. "Le Soleil placé en abîme," 167, 168–69:

Le Soleil, la main ouverte : aïeul prodigue, magnificent. Semeur. . . . Sous sa chaude caresse, ce vieillard prodigue abuse de ses descendants, précipite le cours de leur vie, exalte puis délabre physiquement leurs corps. . . .

Chaque chose porte écusson parti d'argent et de sable.

Dans la tristesse, dans le morne (temps gris, nuageux, sans soleil), la vie comporte plus d'egalité.

L'ombre a toujours une forme, celle du corps qui la porte.

Elle est le lieu de la tristesse infligée par la joie frappant un corps.

Elle est la prison (mouvante), le lieu géométrique de la punition (involontaire) d'une région de l'espace par une autre en joie (ou en gloire).

Enfin, elle est d'autant plus sombre que la joie est plus forte (éblouissante).

Mais cette punition est éphémère, ou du moins change-ante, capricieuse. «Chacun son tour», pourrait-on dire. Et voilà qui peut la rendre supportable.

En somme, dans le même instant que le soleil frappe de joie une chose, il l'oblige à assumer sa responsabilité, et chaque chose alors condamne — et exécute le jugement, la punition.

Le soleil, qui la gifle de joie, affuble du même coup chaque chose de sa noire robe de juge.

33. Albert Camus, *The Myth of Sisyphus and Other Essays*, trans. by Justin O'Brien, 38. *Le Mythe de Sisyphe*, 74: Si j'étais arbre parmi les arbres, chat parmi les animaux, cette vie aurait un sens ou plutôt ce problème n'en aurait point car je ferais partie de ce monde. Je *serais* ce monde auquel je m'oppose maintenant par toute ma conscience et par tout mon exigence de familiarité. . . . Et qu'est-ce qui fait le fond de ce conflit, de cette fracture entre le monde et mon esprit, sinon la conscience que j'en ai?

34. "Le Soleil placé en abîme," III, 170: L'obscurité froide (et acide) est la seule chose qui puisse me faire prendre le soleil en bonne part.

35. "Le Soleil placé en abîme," 165:

Le plus proche et le plus tyrannique, certes.

Mais enfin, l'un seulement des soleils.

36. "Le Soleil placé en abîme," 177, 178:

C'est une artillerie qui, brusquement charmée, a tourné à
l'horlogerie.

Une artillerie dont les boulets sont devenus rouages . . .
l'harmonieux fonctionnement et au silence, ou plutôt au
murmure, au ronronnement du plein-jeu?

37. "Le Soleil placé en abîme," 179: Pourquoi le soleil n'est-il
pas un objet? Parce que c'est lui-même qui . . . tue . . . les sujets qui le regardent comme objet.

38. "Le Soleil placé en abîme," 165–66:

Recommencer volontairement l'hymne. Prendre décidé-
ment le soleil en bonne part. C'est aussi là le pouvoir du
langage. Nous en féliciter, réjouir. L'en féliciter. L'honorer,
le chanter, tâchant seulement de *renouveler* les thèmes (et
variations) de ce los. Le nuancer, en plein ravissement. . . .

Il faut donc métalogiquement le «refaire», le posséder.

En plein ravissement. . . .

Changer le mal en bien. Les travaux forcés en Paradis.

Puis finir dans l'ambiguïté hautement dédaigneuse, ironi-
que et tonique à la fois; le fonctionnement verbal, sans aucun
coefficient laudatif ni péjoratif : l'objeu.

39. "Le Soleil placé en abîme," 173:

le répit, . . . les vacances du bourreau.

La vie commune avec une étoile . . .

notes to chapter 4.

1. "For Leonie Zacharias," *Poems 1906 to 1926*, trans. by J. B.
Leishman, 258. "Für Leonie Zacharias," in *Sämtliche Werke*, II,
249:

Oh sage, Dichter, was du tust?
　　　　　　　　　　— Ich rühme.
Aber das Tödliche und Ungetüme,
wie hältst du's aus, wie nimmst du's hin?
　　　　　　　　　　— Ich rühme.
Aber das Namenlose, Anonyme,
wie rufst du's, Dichter, dennoch an?
　　　　　　　　　　— Ich rühme.
Woher dein Recht, in jeglichem Kostüme,
in jeder Maske wahr zu sein?
　　　　　　　　　　— Ich rühme.
Und daß das Stille und das Ungestüme
wie Stern und Sturm dich kennen?
　　　　　　　　　:— weil ich rühme.

2. *Letters to Merline, 1919–1922*, trans. by Violet M. Macdonald,
48–49. *Rainer Maria Rilke et Merline: Correspondance 1920–
1926*, 92–93: l'Art, tel que je le conçois, est un mouvement contre

nature. . . . Si c'est l'idée du sacrifice que le moment du plus grand danger coincide avec celui où on est sauvé, il n'y a certainement rien qui ressemble plus au sacrifice que cette terrible volonté de l'Art. . . . Tout ce que les autres oublient, pour se rendre la vie possible, nous allons toujours le découvrir et l'agrandir même. . . . A moins qu'on donne à l'acte de la victoire un sens mystérieux et beaucoup plus profond, ce n'est pas à nous de nous croire les dompteurs de nos lions intérieurs. —Mais tout à coup nous nous sentons marcher à côté d'eux comme dans un triomphe, sans pouvoir nous rappeler de l'instant même où se faisait cette inconcevable réconciliation (: pont à peine courbé qui relie le terrible au tendre . . .).

3. *Letters of Rainer Maria Rilke, 1910–1926*, trans. by Jane Bannard Greene and M. D. Herter Norton, 325. *Briefe aus Muzot, 1921 bis 1926*, 186: Die Anschauung, sündig zu sein und des Loskaufs zu bedürfen als Voraussetzung zu Gott, widersteht immer mehr einem Herzen, das die Erde begriffen hat.

4. *Letters of Rainer Marie Rilke, 1892–1910*, trans. by Jane Bannard Greene and M. D. Herter Norton, 111. *Rainer Maria Rilke-Lou Andreas-Salomé, Briefwechsel*, 58: Es riß mich aus mir heraus . . . durch alle ihre beladenen Leben. Ich mußte mir oft laut sagen, daß ich nicht einer von ihnen bin, daß ich wieder fortgehen würde aus dieser schrecklichen Stadt, in der sie sterben werden. . . .

5. My translation from *Die Aufzeichnungen des Malte Laurids Brigge, Werke; Auswahl in Zwei Bänden: Prosa*, II, 46. Rilke's source for this is Baudelaire, *Oeuvres*, I, 241: que je ne suis pas inférieur à ceux que je méprise.

6. *Letters of Rainer Marie Rilke, 1910–1926*, 277. *Briefe aus Muzot*, 67: in der vollkommenen Weite des Weltalls ist es: eine Richtung des Herzens.

7. "The Young Workman's Letter," *Selected Works: Prose*, trans. by G. Craig Houston, 69. "Der Brief des jungen Arbeiters," *Werke*, II, 334: Wird der Tod wirklich durchsichtiger durch diese hinter ihn verschleppten Lichtquellen?

8. "The seventh elegy," *Duino Elegies*, trans. by J. B. Leishman and Stephen Spender, 63. "Die siebente Elegie," *Sämtliche Werke*, I, 712:

Enterbte,
denen das Frühere nicht und noch nicht das Nächste gehört.

9. *The Notebooks of Malte Laurids Brigge*, 51. *Werke*, II, 45: Wenn meine Furcht nicht so groß wäre, so würde ich mich damit trösten, daß es nicht unmöglich ist, alles anders zu sehen und doch zu leben.

10. *Letters of Rainer Maria Rilke, 1910–1926*, 162. *Briefe aus den Jahren 1914 bis 1921*, 151: Diese Zustände des Erstarrens kön-

nen ja leicht Verwandlungen sein, innere Umbauten, auf die ein erneutes Dastehen und Sich-Fühlen folgt, wenn der Umbau geschehen ist . . .

11. "Baudelaire," *Poems 1906 to 1926*, 256. "Baudelaire," *Sämtliche Werke*, II, 246:

> Der Dichter einzig hat die Welt geeinigt,
> die weit in jedem auseinanderfällt.
>
> Das Schöne hat er unerhört bescheinigt,
> doch da er selbst noch feiert, was ihn peinigt,
> hat er unendlich den Ruin gereinigt:
>
> und auch noch das Vernichtende wird Welt.

12. *Letters of Rainer Marie Rilke, 1910–1926*, 373. *Briefe aus Muzot*, 332–33: Der Tod ist die uns abgekehrte, von uns unbeschienene *Seite des Lebens. . . . es gibt weder ein Diesseits noch Jenseits, sondern die große Einheit.* . . .

13. *Letters of Rainer Maria Rilke, 1910–1926*, 342. *Briefe aus Muzot*, 280–81: So ausgedehnt das „Außen" ist, es verträgt mit allen seinen siderischen Distanzen kaum einen Vergleich mit den Dimensionen, *mit der Tiefendimension unseres Inneren*, das nicht einmal die Geräumigkeit des Weltalls nötig hat, um in sich fast unabsehlich zu sein. . . . Mir stellt es sich immer mehr so dar, als ob unser gebräuchliches Bewußtsein die Spitze einer Pyramide bewohne, deren Basis in uns (und gewissermaßen unter uns) so völlig in die Breite geht, daß wir, je weiter wir in sie niederzulassen uns befähigt sehen, desto allgemeiner einbezogen erscheinen in die von Zeit und Raum unabhängigen Gegebenheiten des irdischen, des, im weitesten Begriffe, *weltischen* Daseins. Ich habe seit meiner frühesten Jugend die Vermutung empfunden (und hab ihr auch, wo ich dafür ausreichte, nachgelebt), daß in einem tieferen Durchschnitt dieser Bewußtseinspyramide uns das einfache *Sein* könnte zum Ereignis werden, jenes unverbrüchliche Vorhanden-Sein und Zugleich-Sein alles dessen, was an der oberen „normalen" Spitze des Selbstbewußtseins nur als „Ablauf" zu erleben verstattet ist.

14. "The eighth elegy," *Duino Elegies*, 69. "Die achte Elegie," *Sämtliche Werke*, 1, 715:

> Und wo wir Zukunft sehn, dort sieht es Alles
> und sich in Allem und geheilt für immer.

15. "Everything Beckons to Us to Perceive It," *Poems 1906 to 1926*, 193. "Es winkt zu Fühlung fast aus allen Dingen," *Sämtliche Werke*, II, 93:

> Durch alle Wesen reicht der *eine* Raum:
> Weltinnenraum. Die Vögel fliegen still
> durch uns hindurch. O, der ich wachsen will,
> ich seh hinaus, und *in* mir wächst der Baum.

16. "The Stranger," *Selected Works: Poetry*, trans. by J. B. Leishman, 184. "Der Fremde," *Sämtliche Werke*, I, 627:

> tiefer wissend, daß man nirgends bleibt;
> und schon sah er bei dem nächsten Biegen
> wieder Wege, Brücken, Länder liegen
> bis an Städte, die man übertreibt,

> Und dies alles immer unbegehrend
> hinzulassen, schien ihm mehr als seines
> Lebens Lust, Besitz und Ruhm.

17. "To Lou Andreas-Salomé," *Poems 1906 to 1926*, 127–28. "An Lou Andreas-Salomé," *Sämtliche Werke*, II, 39–40:

> Entsinnen ist da nicht genug, es muß
> von jenen Augenblicken pures Dasein
> auf meinem Grunde sein, ein Niederschlag
> der unermeßlich überfüllten Lösung.
> Denn ich *gedenke* nicht, das, was ich *bin*
> rührt mich um deinetwillen.

18. *Letters of Rainer Maria Rilke, 1892–1910*, 121. *Rainer Maria Rilke-Lou Andreas-Salomé, Briefwechsel*, 88–89: wo ich schaffe bin ich wahr und ich möchte die Kraft finden, mein Leben ganz auf diese Wahrheit zu gründen, . . . die mir manchmal gegeben ist.

19. "The Spanish Trilogy," *Poems 1906 to 1926*, 134–35. "Die Spanische Trilogie," *Sämtliche Werke*, II, 43–44:

> Aus dieser Wolke, siehe: die den Stern
> so wild verdeckt, der eben war – (und mir),
> auf diesem Bergland drüben, das jetzt Nacht,
> Nachtwinde hat für eine Zeit – (und mir),
> aus diesem Fluß im Talgrund, der den Schein
> zerrissner Himmels-Lichtung fängt – (und mir);
> aus mir und alledem ein einzig Ding
> zu machen, Herr: aus mir und dem Gefühl,
> mit dem die Herde, eingekehrt im Pferch,
> das große dunkle Nichtmehrsein der Welt
> ausatmend hinnimmt–, mir und jedem Licht
> im Finstersein der vielen Häuser, Herr:
> ein Ding zu machen; aus den Fremden, denn
> nicht Einen kenn ich, Herr, und mir und mir
> *ein* Ding zu machen; aus den Schlafenden,
> den fremden alten Männern im Hospiz,
> die wichtig in den Betten husten, aus
> schlaftrunknen Kindern an so fremder Brust,
> aus vielen Ungenaun und immer mir,
> aus nichts als mir und dem, was ich nicht kenn,
> das Ding zu machen, Herr Herr Herr, das Ding,
> das welthaft-irdisch wie ein Meteor

in seiner Schwere nur die Summe Flugs
zusammennimmt: nichts wiegend als die Ankunft.
20. "The Spanish Trilogy," *Poems 1906 to 1926*, 135. "Die Spanische Trilogie," *Sämtliche Werke*, II, 44–45:

> Warum muß einer gehn und fremde Dinge
> so auf sich nehmen, wie vielleicht der Träger
> den fremdlings mehr und mehr gefüllten Marktkorb
> von Stand zu Stand hebt und beladen nachgeht
> und kann nicht sagen: Herr, wozu das Gastmahl?
>
> Warum muß einer dastehn wie ein Hirt,
> so ausgesetzt dem Übermaß von Einfluß,
> beteiligt so an diesem Raum voll Vorgang,
> daß er gelehnt an einen Baum der Landschaft
> sein Schicksal hätte, ohne mehr zu handeln.
> Und hat doch nicht im viel zu großen Blick
> die stille Milderung der Herde. Hat
> nichts als Welt, hat Welt in jedem Aufschaun,
> in jeder Neigung Welt. Ihm dringt, was andern
> gerne gehört, unwirtlich wie Musik
> und blind ins Blut und wandelt sich vorüber.
>
> Da steht er nächstens auf und hat den Ruf
> des Vogels draußen schon in seinem Dasein
> und fühlt sich kühn, weil er die ganzen Sterne
> in sein Gesicht nimmt, schwer—, o nicht wie einer,
> der der Geliebten diese Nacht bereitet
> und sie verwöhnt mit den gefühlten Himmeln.

21. *Letters to Merline*, 47. *Rainer Marie Rilke et Merline*, 91: . . .
on doit arriver comme on arrive parmi les morts, en remettant
toutes les forces entre la main de l'Ange qui nous conduit.
22. "The eighth elegy," *Duino Elegies*, 67. "Die achte Elegie,"
Sämtliche Werke, I, 714:

> Immer ist es Welt
> und niemals Nirgends ohne Nicht. . . .

23. "The Spanish Trilogy," *Poems 1906 to 1926*, 135–36. "Die
Spanische Trilogie," *Sämtliche Werke*, II, 45–46:

> Daß mir doch, wenn ich wieder der Städte Gedräng
> und verwickelten Lärmknäul und die
> Wirrsal des Fahrzeugs um mich habe, einzeln,
> daß mir doch über das dichte Getrieb
> Himmel erinnerte und der erdige Bergrand,
> den von drüben heimwärts die Herde betrat.
> Steinig sei mir zu Mut
> und das Tagwerk des Hirten scheine mir möglich,
> wie er einhergeht und bräunt und mit messendem Steinwurf

seine Herde besäumt, wo sie sich ausfranst.
Langsamen Schrittes, nicht leicht, nachdenklichen
                                        Körpers,
aber im Stehn ist er herrlich. Noch immer dürfte ein Gott
heimlich in diese Gestalt und würde nicht minder.
Abwechselnd weilt er und zieht, wie selber der Tag,
und Schatten der Wolken
durchgehn ihn, als dächte der Raum
langsam Gedanken für ihn.

Sei er wer immer für euch. Wie das wehende Nachtlicht
in den Mantel der Lampe stell ich mich innen in ihn.
Ein Schein wird ruhig. Der Tod
fände sich reiner zurecht.

24. *Letters of Rainer Maria Rilke, 1892–1910,* 118. *Rainer Marie Rilke-Lou Andreas-Salomé, Briefwechsel,* 83: stumpf . . . und hart gegen das Unwichtige und, wie von einer alten Rinde umgeben, steht er unter den Menschen. Aber . . . ganz offen ist er wenn er bei Dingen ist, oder wo Tiere und Menschen ihn still und wie Dinge berühren.

25. "For Count Karl Lanckoroński," *Poems 1906 to 1926,* 352. "Geschrieben für Karl Grafen Lanckoroński," *Sämtliche Werke,* II, 277:

Sie müssen dastehn wie der Hirt, der dauert;
von ferne kann es scheinen, daß er trauert,
im Näherkommen fühlt man wie er wacht.
Und wie für ihn der Gang der Sterne laut ist,
muß ihnen nah sein, wie es ihm vertraut ist,
was schweigend steigt und wandelt in der Nacht.

26. "The Bowl of Roses," *Selected Works: Poetry,* 195–96. "Die Rosenschale," *Sämtliche Werke,* I, 552–53:

Lautloses Leben, Aufgehn ohne Ende,
Raum-brauchen ohne Raum von jenem Raum
zu nehmen, den die Dinge rings verringern,
fast nicht Umrissen-sein wie Ausgespartes
und lauter Inneres, viel seltsam Zartes
und Sich-bescheinendes — bis an den Rand:
ist irgend etwas uns bekannt wie dies?

27. "The Bowl of Roses," *Selected Works: Poetry,* 195. "Die Rosenschale," *Sämtliche Werke,* I, 553:

als ob sie, zehnfach schlafend,
zu dämpfen hätten eines Innern Sehkraft.
Und dies vor allem: daß durch diese Blätter
das Licht hindurch muß. Aus den tausend Himmeln
filtern sie langsam jenen Tropfen Dunkel,
in dessen Feuerschein das wirre Bündel
der Staubgefäße sich erregt und aufbäumt.

28. "R.M.R.," *Selected Works: Poetry*, 354. "Rose, oh reiner Widerspruch, Lust," *Sämtliche Werke*, II, 185:
> Rose, oh reiner Widerspruch, Lust,
> Niemandes Schlaf zu sein unter soviel
> Lidern.

29. "The Bowl of Roses," *Selected Works: Poetry*, 196. "Die Rosenschale," *Sämtliche Werke*, I, 553:
> Und die Bewegung in den Rosen, sieh:
> Gebärden von so kleinem Ausschlagswinkel,
> daß sie unsichtbar blieben, liefen ihre
> Strahlen nicht auseinander in das Weltall.

30. "The Bowl of Roses," *Selected Works: Poetry*, 196. "Die Rosenschale," *Sämtliche Werke*, I, 553:
> die errötende, die wie verwirrt
> nach einer kühlen sich hinüberwendet,
> und wie die kühle fühllos sich zurückzieht,
> und wie die kalte steht, in sich gehüllt,
> unter den offenen, die alles abtun.

31. "The Bowl of Roses," *Selected Works: Poetry*, 196. "Die Rosenschale," *Sämtliche Werke*, I, 554:
> die Welt da draußen
> und Wind und Regen und Geduld des Frühlings
> und Schuld und Unruh und vermummtes Schicksal
> und Dunkelheit der abendlichen Erde
> bis auf der Wolken Wandel, Flucht und Anflug,
> bis auf den vagen Einfluß ferner Sterne
> in eine Hand voll Innres zu verwandeln.

> Nun liegt es sorglos in den offnen Rosen.

32. *Letters of Rainer Maria Rilke, 1892–1910*, 260. *Briefe aus den Jahren 1906 bis 1907*, 200: Das ist es, was wir zu lernen haben, auf gewisse Dinge *nicht* achtgeben; *zu* gesammelt sein, um an sie, an die man nie mit dem ganzen Wesen heran kann, mit irgendeiner empfindlichen Seite zu rühren. My italics.

33. "Turning," *Poems 1906 to 1926*, 183–84. "Wendung," *Sämtliche Werke*, II, 82–84:
> *Der Weg von der Innigkeit zur Größe*
> *geht durch das Opfer.*
> > *Kassner.*

> Lange errang ers im Anschaun.
> Sterne brachen ins Knie
> unter dem ringenden Aufblick.
> Oder er anschaute knieend,
> und seines Instands Duft
> machte ein Göttliches müd,
> daß es ihm lächelte schlafend.

Türme schaute er so,
daß sie erschraken:
wieder sie bauend, hinan, plötzlich, in Einem!
Aber wie oft, die vom Tag
überladene Landschaft
ruhete hin in sein stilles Gewahren, abends.

Tiere traten getrost
in den offenen Blick, weidende,
und die gefangenen Löwen
starrten hinein wie in unbegreifliche Freiheit;
Vögel durchflogen ihn grad,
den gemütigen; Blumen
wiederschauten in ihn
groß wie in Kinder.

        Und das Gerücht, daß ein Schauender sei,
rührte die minder,
fraglicher Sichtbaren,
rührte die Frauen.

Schauend wie lang?
Seit wie lange schon innig entbehrend,
flehend im Grunde des Blicks?

Wenn er, ein Wartender, saß in der Fremde; des Gasthofs
zerstreutes, abgewendetes Zimmer
mürrisch um sich, und im vermiedenen Spiegel
wieder das Zimmer
und später vom quälenden Bett aus
wieder:
da beriets in der Luft,
unfaßbar beriet es
über sein fühlbares Herz,
über sein durch den schmerzhaft verschütteten Körper
dennoch fühlbares Herz
beriet es und richtete:
daß es der Liebe nicht habe.

(Und verwehrte ihm weitere Weihen.)

Denn des Anschauns, siehe, ist eine Grenze.
Und die geschautere Welt
will in der Liebe gedeihn.

Werk des Gesichts ist getan,
tue nun Herz-Werk

an den Bildern in dir, jenen gefangenen; denn du
überwältigtest sie: aber nun kennst du sie nicht.
Siehe, innerer Mann, dein inneres Mädchen,
dieses errungene aus
tausend Naturen, dieses
erst nur errungene, nie
noch geliebte Geschöpf.

34. *Letters of Rainer Maria Rilke, 1910–1926,* 238–39. *Briefe aus den Jahren 1914 bis 1921,* 362: Mit ihm verschiebt sich die Skala, denn er . . . gehört bereits zu jener Welt, in der Höhe — Tiefe ist. . . . See also "For Count Karl Lanckoroński," *Poems 1906 to 1926,* 352:

another measure for the whole creation
is given us in those right-angled knees.

"Geschrieben für Karl Grafen Lanckoroński," *Sämtliche Werke,* II, 277.

so ist der Welt ein neues Maß gegeben
mit diesem rechten Winkel ihres Knie's!

35. *Letters of Rainer Maria Rilke, 1910–1926,* 145. *Briefe aus den Jahren 1914 bis 1921,* 80: Die „Arbeit nach der Natur" hat mir das Seiende in so hohem Grade zur A u f g a b e gemacht, daß mich nur sehr selten noch, wie aus Versehen, ein Ding gewährend und gebend anspricht, ohne die Anforderung in mir gleichwertig und bedeutend hervorgebracht zu sein.

36. *Letters of Rainer Maria Rilke, 1910–1926,* 82. *Rainer Maria Rilke-Lou Andreas-Salomé, Briefwechsel,* 284: . . . jetzt sitz ich da und schau und schau bis mir die Augen wehthun, und . . . sag mirs vor als sollt ichs auswendig lernen und habs doch nicht. . . .

37. "Turning," *Poems 1906 to 1926,* 184. "Wendung," *Sämtliche Werke,* II, 417:
Daß dieses leerzehrende Aus mir hinausschaun
abgelöst werde durch ein liebevolles Bemühtsein
um die innere Fülle.

38. "The ninth elegy," *Duino Elegies,* 77. Die neunte Elegie, *Sämtliche Werke,* I, 719:

ganz im unsichtbarn Herzen verwandeln
in — o unendlich — in uns!

39. Sonnet VI, Part 2, *Sonnets to Orpheus,* trans. by M. D. Herter Norton, 81. *Sämtliche Werke,* I, 754:

Seit Jahrhunderten ruft uns dein Duft
seine süßesten Namen herüber;
plötzlich liegt er wie Ruhm in der Luft.

40. *Letters of Rainer Maria Rilke, 1910–1926,* 292. *Rainer Maria Rilke-Lou Andreas-Salomé, Briefwechsel,* 465: — Was ist Zeit? — *Wann* ist Gegenwart? Über so viel Jahre sprang er mir, mit seinem

völligen Glück, ins weitoffne Gefühl.
41. *Letters of Rainer Marie Rilke, 1910–1926*, 328. *Briefe aus Muzot*, 198: Daß doch nichts verloren geht!
42. Sonnet IV, Part 1, *Sonnets to Orpheus*, 23. *Sämtliche Werke*, I, 733:

> O ihr Zärtlichen, tretet zuweilen
> in den Atem, der euch nicht meint,
> laßt ihn an eueren Wangen sich teilen,
> hinter euch zittert er, wieder vereint.
>
> O ihr Seligen, o ihr Heilen,
> die ihr der Anfang der Herzen scheint.
> Bogen der Pfeile und Ziele von Pfeilen,
> ewiger glänzt euer Lächeln verweint.
>
> Fürchtet euch nicht zu leiden, die Schwere,
> gebt sie zurück an der Erde Gewicht;
> schwer sind die Berge, schwer sind die Meere.
>
> Selbst die als Kinder ihr pflanztet, die Bäume,
> wurden zu schwer längst; ihr trüget sie nicht.
> Aber die Lüfte . . . aber die Räume. . . .

notes to chapter 5.

1. "Reunion Under New Flags," *Residence on Earth and Other Poems*, trans. by Angel Flores, 205. "Reunión bajo las nuevas banderas," *Obras completas*, 251.

> no busco asilo
> en los huecos del llanto: muestro
> la cepa de la abeja: pan radiante
> para el hijo del hombre . . .

2. "Diver," *Selected Poems of Pablo Neruda*, trans. by Ben Belitt, 233. "Oda al buzo," *Obras completas*, 1322:

> ¿ aprendí que ser buzo
> es un oficio
> difícil? ¡No!
> Infinito.

3. My translation of "El hombre invisible" ("The Invisible Man"), *Obras completas*, 940:

> Dadme para mi vida,
> todas las vidas,
> dadme todo el dolor
> de todo el mundo, . . .

4. "Let the Rail Splitter Awake," trans. by Waldeen, in *Let the Rail Splitter Awake and Other Poems*, 40. "Que despierte el leñador," *Obras completas*, 509:

Yo vine aquí para cantar
y para que cantes conmigo.

5. "Things Breaking," *Selected Poems*, 279. "Oda a las cosas volas,"
Obras completas, 1580:

La vida va moliendo
vidrios, gastando ropas,
haciendo añicos,
triturando
formas.

6. "Albert Rojas Jiménez Comes Flying," *Selected Poems*, 89.
"Alberto Rojas Jiménez viene volando," *Obras completas*, 226–27:

Entre plumas que asustan, entre noches,
entre magnolias, entre telegramas,
entre el viento del Sur y el Oeste marino,
            vienes volando.

. . . .

Sobre diputaciones y farmacias,
y ruedas, y abogados, y navíos,
y dientes rojos recién arrancados,
            vienes volando.

7. "Death Alone," *Residence on Earth*, 51. "Sólo la muerte,"
Obras completas, 199:

Yo veo, solo, a veces,
ataúdes a vela
zarpar con difuntos pálidos, con mujeres de trenzas muertas,
con panaderos blancos como ángeles,
con niñas pensativas casadas con notarios,
ataúdes subiendo el río vertical de los muertos,
el río morado,
hacia arriba, con las velas hinchadas por el sonido de la muerte,
hinchadas por el sonido silencioso de la muerte.

8. "Ritual of My Legs," *Selected Poems*, 73. "Ritual de mis piernas," *Obras completas*, 186:

. . . la vida termina definitivamente en mis pies,
lo extranjero y lo hostil allí comienza.

9. "Unity," *Residence on Earth*, 21. "Unidad," *Obras completas*,
165:

las cosas de cuero, de madera, de lana,

. . . .

se unen en torno a mí como paredes.

10. *Nausea*, trans. by Lloyd Alexander, 171–72. *La Nausée*, 162:
Et puis voilà : tout d'un coup, c'était là, c'était clair comme le
jour : l'existence s'était soudain dévoilée. Elle avait perdu son
allure inoffensive de catégorie abstraite : c'était la pâte même des
choses, cette racine était pétrie dans de l'existence. Ou plutôt la
racine, les grilles du jardin, le banc, le gazon rare de la pelouse,

tout ça s'était évanoui; la diversité des choses, leur individualité
n'étaient qu'une apparence, un vernis. Ce vernis avait fondu, il
restait des masses monstrueuses et molles, en désordre — nues
d'une effrayante et obscène nudité.

11. Translation, used by permission, from unpublished manuscript of Victor Perera. "Walking Around," *Obras completas*,
204–5:

Sucede que me canso de ser hombre.
Sucede que entro en las sastrerías y en los cines
marchito, impenetrable, como un cisne de fieltro
navegando en un agua de origen y ceniza.

El olor de las peluquerías me hace llorar a gritos.
Sólo quiero un descanso de piedras o de lana,
sólo quiero no ver establecimientos ni jardines,
ni mercaderías, ni anteojos, ni ascensores.

Sucede que me canso de mis pies y mis uñas
y mi pelo y mi sombra.
Sucede que me canso de ser hombre.

Sin embargo sería delicioso
asustar a un notario con un lirio cortado
o dar muerte a una monja con un golpe de oreja.
Sería bello
ir por las calles con un cuchillo verde
y dando gritos hasta morir de frío.

No quiero seguir siendo raíz en las tinieblas,
vacilante, extendido, tiritando de sueño,
hacia abajo, en las tapias mojadas de la tierra,
absorbiendo y pensando, comiendo cada día.

No quiero para mí tantas desgracias.
No quiero continuar de raíz y de tumba,
de subterráneo solo, de bodega con muertos,
aterido, muriéndome de pena.

Por eso el día lunes arde como el petróleo
cuando me ve llegar con mi cara de cárcel,
y aúlla en su transcurso como una rueda herida,
y da pasos de sangre caliente hacia la noche.

Y me empuja a ciertos rincones, a ciertas casas húmedas
a hospitales donde los huesos salen por la ventana,

a ciertas zapaterías con olor a vinagre,
a calles espantosas como grietas.

Hay pájaros de color de azufre y horribles intestinos
colgando de las puertas de las casas que odio,
hay dentaduras olvidadas en una cafetera,
hay espejos
que debieran haber llorado de vergüenza y espanto,
hay paraguas en todas partes, y venenos, y ombligos.

Yo paseo con calma, con ojos, con zapatos,
con furia, con olvido,
paso, cruzo oficinas y tiendas de ortopedia,
y patios donde hay ropas colgadas de un alambre:
calzoncillos, toallas y camisas que lloran
lentas lágrimas sucias.

12. "Ritual of My Legs," *Selected Poems*, 71. "Ritual de mis piernas," *Obras completas*, 186:

Tienen existencia los trajes, color, forma, designio,
y profundo lugar en nuestros mitos, demasiado lugar,
demasiados muebles y demasiadas habitaciones hay en el mundo,
y mi cuerpo vive entre y bajo tantas cosas abatido,
con un pensamiento fijo de esclavitud y de cadenas.

13. "Viajes al corazón de Quevedo y por las costas del mundo," *Viajes*, 18: Si ya hemos muerto, si venimos de la profunda crisis, perderemos el temor a la muerte.

14. "Signifying Shadows," *Residence on Earth*, 47. "Significa sombras," *Obras completas*, 193:

Ay, que lo que yo soy siga existiendo y cesando de existir,
y que mi obediencia se ordene con tales condiciones de hierro
que el temblor de las muertes y de los nacimientos no conmueva
el profundo sitio que quiero reservar para mí eternamente.

Sea, pues, lo que soy, en alguna parte y en todo tiempo,
establecido y asegurado y ardiente testigo,
cuidadosamente destruyéndose y preservándose incesantemente,
evidentemente empeñado en su deber original.

15. "The Dictators," *Selected Poems*, 161. "Los Dictadores," *Obras completas*, 485:

Ha quedado un olor entre los cañaverales:
una mezcla de sangre y cuerpo, un penetrante
pétalo nauseabundo.
Entre los cocoteros las tumbas están llenas

de huesos demolidos, de estertores callados.
El delicado sátrapa conversa
con copas, cuellos y cordones de oro.
El pequeño palacio brilla como un reloj
y las rápidas risas enguantadas
atraviesan a veces los pasillos
y se reúnen a las voces muertas
y a las bocas azules frescamente enterradas.
El llanto está escondido como una planta
cuya semilla cae sin cesar sobre el suelo
y hace crecer sin luz sus grandes hojas ciegas.
El odio se ha formado escama a escama,
golpe a golpe, en el agua terrible del pantano,
con un hocico lleno de légamo y silencio.

16. Ezra Pound, "Dr. Williams' Position," *The Dial*, 85 (November, 1928), 398.

17. "Carl Sandburg's Complete Poems," *Selected Essays of William Carlos Williams*, 277.

18. "The Dead in the Square," trans. by Robert Brittain, in *Let the Rail Splitter Awake*, 47. "Los muertos de la plaza (*28 de enero 1946, Santiago de Chile*)," *Obras completas*, 437:

    No quiero que me den la mano
    empapada con nuestra sangre.
    Pido castigo.

19. "The Dead in the Square," 44; 468:

    Yo escuché una voz que venía
    desde el fondo estrecho del pique,
    como de un útero infernal,
    y después asomar arriba
    una criatura sin rostro,
    una máscara polvorienta
    de sudor, de sangre y de polvo.

    Y ése me dijo: "Adonde vayas,
    habla tú de estos tormentos,
    habla tú, hermano, de tu hermano
    que vive abajo, en el infierno."

20. "Let the Rail Splitter Awake," trans. by Waldeen, in *Let the Rail Splitter Awake*, 32–33. "Que despierte el leñador," *Obras completas*, 544:

            Tú eres
    lo que soy, lo que fuí, lo que debemos
    amparar, el fraternal subsuelo
    de América purísima, los sencillos
    hombres de los caminos y las calles.
    Mi hermano Juan vende zapatos

como tu hermano John,
mi hermana Juana pela papas,
como tu prima Jane,
y mi sangre es minera y marinera
como tu sangre, Peter.

21. Walt Whitman, "Prefaces to 'Leaves of Grass,'" *Complete Prose Works*, 259.
22. "Oda a la claridad" ("Ode to Clarity"), *Obras completas*, 966:
Vivo,
amo
y soy amado.
23. My translation of "El hombre invisible" ("The Invisible Man"), *Obras completas*, 938–39:
yo quiero
que todos vivan
en mi vida
y canten en mi canto,
yo no tengo importancia,
no tengo tiempo
para mis asuntos,
de noche y de día
debo anotar lo que pasa,
y no olvidar a nadie.
24. "Infancia y poesía," ("Infancy and Poetry"), *Obras completas*, 18:
Se aprende la poesía paso a paso entre las cosas y los seres, sin
apartarlos sino agregándolos a todos en una ciega extensión
del amor.
25. "The Fugitive," trans. by Waldeen, in *Let the Rail Splitter Awake*, 69. "El fugitivo," *Obras completas*, 564:
soy sólo
pueblo, puerta escondida, pan oscuro,
y cuando me recibes, te recibes
a ti mismo, a ese huésped
tantas veces golpeado
y tantas veces
renacido.
26. "Our Duty Toward Life" (speech given at the Continental Peace Congress in 1949 in Mexico City), trans. by Joseph M. Bernstein, in *Let the Rail Splitter Awake*, 12, 14.
27. "La casa de las odas" ("The House of Odes"), *Obras completas*, 999, 1000:
Quiero . . .

. . . .

que todo sea
taza o herramienta.

. . . .

Para que todos vivan
en ella
hago mi casa
con odas
transparentes.

28. "From: Elephant," *Selected Poems*, 293, 295. "Oda al elefante,"
Obras completas, 1583–84:

Espesa bestia pura,
San Elefante,
animal santo
del bosque sempiterno,
todo materia fuerte
fina
y equilibrada,
cuero
de
talabartería planetaria,
marfil
compacto, satinado,
sereno
como
la carne de la luna,
ojos mínimos
para mirar, no para ser mirados,
y trompa
tocadora,
corneta
del contacto,
manguera
del
animal
gozoso
en
su
frescura,
máquina movediza,
teléfono del bosque,
y así
pasa tranquilo
y bamboleante
con su vieja envoltura,
con su ropaje
de árbol arrugado,
su pantalón
caído
y su colita.

29. "From: Elephant," *Selected Poems*, 295–97; 1584–85:
No nos equivoquemos.
La dulce y grande bestia de la selva
no es el clown,
sino el padre
el padre en la luz verde,
es el antiguo
y puro
progenitor terrestre.

Total fecundación,
tantálica
codicia,
fornicación
y piel
mayoritaria,
costumbres
en la lluvia
rodearon
el reino
de los elefantes,
y fue
con sal
y sangre
la genérica guerra
en el silencio.

Las escamosas formas,
el lagarto león,
el pez montaña
el milodonto cíclope,
cayeron,
decayeron,
fueron fermento verde en el pantano,
tesoro
de las tórridas moscas,
de escarabajos crueles.
Emergió el elefante
del miedo destronado.
Fue casi vegetal, oscura torre
del firmamento verde,
y de hojas dulces, miel
y agua de roca
se alimentó su estirpe.

30. *Letters of Rainer Maria Rilke, 1910–1926*, trans. by Jane Bannard Greene and M. D. Herter Norton, 197. *Briefe aus den Jahren 1914 bis 1921*, 249:

Wenn der Mensch doch aufhörte, sich auf die Grausamkeit in
der Natur zu berufen, um seine eigene zu entschuldigen! Er
vergißt, wie unendlich schuldlos auch noch das Fürchterlichste
in der Natur geschieht, sie sieht ihm nicht zu, sie hat keine
Distanz dazu, — sie *i s t* im Entsetzlichsten ganz, auch ihre
Fruchtbarkeit ist darin, ihre Großmut—; es [ist], wenn man so
sagen soll, auch nichts anderes als ein Ausdruck ihrer Fülle.
Ihr Bewußtsein besteht in ihrer Vollzähligkeit, weil sie *alles*
enthält, enthält sie auch das Grausame.

31. "Ercilla," *Residence on Earth*, 175. "Ercilla," *Obras completas*,
347. (The first line of the Spanish text noted below is missing in
the text given in *Obras completas*; it is in *Residence on Earth*):

todo será una gota en la espesura,
todo será en la tierra devorado.

. . . .

Todo vuelve al silencio coronado de plumas
en donde un rey remoto devora enredaderas.

32. "A Light from the Sea," *Selected Poems*, 263. "Oda a la luz
marina," *Obras completas*, 1386:

y nos enseñe a ver ola por ola
el mar
y flor a flor la tierra.

33. "Entrance into Wood," *Residence on Earth*, 81, 83. "Entrada
a la madera," *Obras completas*, 217–18:

Con mi razón apenas, con mis dedos,
con lentas aguas lentas inundadas,
caigo al imperio de los nomeolvides,
a una tenaz atmósfera de luto,
a una olvidada sala decaída,
a un racimo de tréboles amargos.

Caigo en la sombra, en medio
de destruídas cosas,
y miro arañas, y apaciento bosques
de secretas maderas inconclusas,
y ando entre húmedas fibras arrancadas
al vivo ser de substancia y silencio.

Dulce materia, oh rosa de alas secas,
en mi hundimiento tus pétalos subo
con pies pesados de roja fatiga,
y en tu catedral dura me arrodillo
golpeándome los labios con un ángel.

Es que soy yo ante tu color de mundo,
ante tus pálidas espadas muertas,

ante tus corazones reunidos,
ante tu silenciosa multitud.

Soy yo ante tu ola de olores muriendo,
envueltos en otoño y resistencia:
soy yo emprendiendo un viaje funerario
entre tus cicatrices amarillas:

soy yo con mis lamentos sin origen,
sin alimentos, desvelado, solo,
entrando oscurecidos corredores,
llegando a tu materia misteriosa.

Veo moverse tus corrientes secas,
veo crecer manos interrumpidas,
oigo tus vegetales oceánicos
crujir de noche y furia sacudidos,
y siento morir hojas hacia adentro,
incorporando materiales verdes
a tu inmovilidad desamparada.

Poros, vetas, círculos de dulzura,
peso, temperatura silenciosa,
flechas pegadas a tu alma caída,
seres dormidos en tu boca espesa,
polvo de dulce pulpa consumida,
ceniza llena de apagadas almas,
venid a mí, a mi sueño sin medida,
caed en mi alcoba en que la noche cae
y cae sin cesar como agua rota,
y a vuestra vida, a vuestra muerte asidme,
a vuestros materiales sometidos,
a vuestras muertas palomas neutrales,
y hagamos fuego, y silencio, y sonido,
y ardamos, y callemos, y campanas.

34. Kenneth Yasuda, *The Japanese Haiku: Its Essential Nature, History, and Possibilities in English, With Selected Examples,* 31, 49.

35. Charles Baudelaire, "Du Vin et du haschisch," *Oeuvres,* I, texte établi et annoté par Y.-G. Le Dantec, 264: Toute contradiction est devenue unité. L'homme est *passé* dieu.

36. "Poets Celestial," in *Selected Poems,* 143. "Los poetas celestes," *Obras completas,* 446:

    . . . qué hicisteis
ante el reinado de la angustia,
frente a este oscuro ser humano,

a esta pateada compostura,
a esta cabeza sumergida
en el estiércol, a esta esencia
de ásperas vidas pisoteadas?

37. My translation of "Oda al pan" ("Ode to Bread"), *Obras completas*, 1061–62:

Pan,
con harina,
aqua
y fuego
te levantas.
Espeso y leve,
recostado y redondo,
repites
el vientre
de la madre,
equinoccial
germinación
terrestre.
Pan,
qué fácil
y qué profundo eres:
en la bandeja blanca
de la panadería
se alargan tus hileras
como utensilios, platos
o papeles,
y de pronto,
la ola
de la vida,
la conjunción del germen
y del fuego,
creces, creces
de pronto
como
cintura, boca, senos,
colinas de la tierra.

38. "Oda al pan," *Obras completas*, 1062–63:

Oh pan de cada boca,
no
te imploraremos,
los hombres
no somos
mendigos
de vagos dioses
o de ángeles oscuros:

del mar y de la tierra
haremos pan,
plantaremos de trigo
la tierra y los planetas,
. . . .
el pan, el pan
para todos los pueblos
y con él lo que tiene
forma y sabor de pan
repartiremos:
la tierra,
la belleza,
el amor,
todo eso
tiene sabor de pan,
forma de pan,
germinación de harina,
todo
nació para ser compartido,
para ser entregado,
para multiplicarse.

39. My translation of "La muerte" ("The Dead"), *Obras completas*, 669:

No compré una parcela del cielo que vendían
los sacerdotes, ni acepté tinieblas
que el metafísico manufacturaba
para despreocupados poderosos.

Quiero estar en la muerte con los pobres
que no tuvieron tiempo de estudiarla,
mientras los apaleaban los que tienen
el cielo dividido y arreglado.

40. "Oda al pan" ("Ode to Bread"), *Obras completas*, 1064:

Iremos coronados
con espigas,
conquistando
tierra y pan para todos,
y entonces
también la vida
tendrá forma de pan,
será simple y profunda,
innumerable y pura.
Todos los seres
tendrán derecho
a la tierra y la vida,
y así será el pan de mañana,

el pan de cada boca,
sagrado,
consagrado,
porque será el producto
de la más larga y dura
lucha humana.

No tiene alas
la victoria terrestre:
tiene pan en sus hombros,
y vuela valerosa
liberando la tierra
como una panadera
conducida en el viento.

41. "The Heights of Macchu Picchu," trans. by Waldeen, in *Let
the Railsplitter Awake*, 77. "Alturas de Macchu Picchu," *Obras
completas*, 313–14:

Cuántas veces en las calles de invierno de una ciudad o en
un autobús o un barco en el crepúsculo, o en la soledad
más espesa, la de la noche de fiesta, bajo el sonido
de sombras y campanas, en la misma gruta del placer humano,
me quise detener a buscar la eterna veta insondable
que antes toqué en la piedra o en el relámpago que el beso
desprendía.

. . . .
No pude asir sino un racimo de rostros o de máscaras
precipitadas, como anillos de oro vacío,
como ropas dispersas hijas de un otoño rabioso
que hiciera temblar el miserable árbol de las razas asustadas.

42. "The Heights of Macchu Picchu," 76, 77; 313:

       La cólera ha extenuado
la triste mercancía del vendedor de seres,
y, mientras en la altura del ciruelo, el rocío
desde mil años deja su carta transparente
sobre la misma rama que lo espera. . . .

43. "The Heights of Macchu Picchu," 78; 314:

y su quebranto aciago de cada día era
como una copa negra que bebían temblando.

44. "The Heights of Macchu Picchu," 79; 315:

No pude amar en cada ser un árbol
con su pequeño otoño a cuestas (la muerte de mil hojas)
todas las falsas muertes y las resurrecciones
sin tierra, sin abismo:

. . . .
rodé muriendo de mi propia muerte.

45. "The Heights of Macchu Picchu," 82; 318:

costumbres, sílabas
raídas, máscaras de luz deslumbradora.
46. "The Heights of Macchu Picchu," 85; 320:
El reino muerto vive todavía.
47. "The Heights of Macchu Picchu," 88; 322, 323:
¡ Devuélveme el esclavo que enterraste!
Sacude de las tierras el pan duro
del miserable, muéstrame los vestidos
del siervo y su ventana.
Dime cómo durmió cuando vivía.

. . . .

¡ y deja que en mí palpite, como un ave mil años prisionera,
el viejo corazón del olvidado!
48. "The Heights of Macchu Picchu," 89, 90, 91; 323, 324:
no veo a la bestia veloz,
no veo el ciego ciclo de sus garras,
veo el antiguo ser, servidor, el dormido
en los campos, veo un cuerpo, mil cuerpos, un hombre, mil
mujeres,

. . . .

Sube a nacer conmigo, hermano.

. . . .

Yo vengo a hablar por vuestra boca muerta.

. . . .

Hablad por mis palabras y mi sangre.
49. "The Fugitive," trans. by Waldeen, in *Let the Railsplitter
Awake,* 70–71. "El Fugitivo," *Obras completas,* 565–66:
No me siento solo en la noche,
en la oscuridad de la tierra.
Soy pueblo, pueblo innumerable.
Tengo en mi voz la fuerza pura
para atravesar el silencio
y germinar en las tinieblas.
Muerte, martirio, sombra, hielo,
cubren de pronto la semilla.
Y parece enterrado el pueblo.
Pero el maíz vuelve a la tierra.
Atravesaron el silencio
sus implacables manos rojas.
Desde la muerte renacemos.

notes to chapter 6.

1. Wallace Stevens, "Asides on the Oboe," *The Collected Poems
of Wallace Stevens,* 251.

2. "Prologue to Kora in Hell," *Selected Essays of William Carlos Williams*, 11–12.

3. "Père Sebastian Rasles," *In the American Grain*, 120.

4. "Comment," *Selected Essays*, 28–29.

5. My translation of "El hombre invisible" ("The Invisible Man"), *Obras completas*, 940:

> Dadme para mi vida,
> todas las vidas,
> dadme todo el dolor
> de todo el mundo,
> yo voy a transformarlo
> en esperanza.
>
> Dadme
> todas las alegrías,
> aun las más secretas,
> porque si así no fuera,
> ¿cómo van a saberse?
> Yo tengo que contarlas,
> dadme
> la lucha
> de cada día
> porque ellas son mi canto,
> y así andaremos juntos,
> codo a codo,
> todos los hombres,
> mi canto los reúne:
> el canto del hombre invisible
> que canta con todos los hombres.

6. *Letters to a Young Poet*, trans. by M. D. Herter Norton, 67. *Rainer Maria Rilke, Briefe, 1897 bis 1914*, 100: Wir müssen unser Dasein so *weit*, als es irgend geht, annehmen; alles, auch das Unerhörte, muß darin möglich sein.

7. "Prologue to Kora in Hell," *Selected Essays*, 17.

8. Gabriel Marcel, *The Philosophy of Existentialism*, trans. by Manya Harari, 38, 15.

9. "El hombre invisible" ("The Invisible Man"), *Obras completas*, 937:

> yo no soy superior
> a mi hermano
> pero sonrío,
> porque voy por las calles
> y sólo yo no existo,
> la vida corre
> como todos los ríos,
> yo soy el único
> invisible,

no hay misteriosas sombras,
no hay tinieblas,
todo el mundo me habla,
me quieren contar cosas,
me hablan de sus parientes,
de sus miserias
y de sus alegrías,
todos pasan y todos
me dicen algo, . . .

suggested reading,
including works cited

I. GENERAL BACKGROUND

Abrahms, M. H., *The Mirror and the Lamp: Romantic Theory and the Critical Tradition*. New York: W. W. Norton & Company, Inc., 1958.

Aiken, Conrad, "The Place of Imagism." *The New Republic*, 3 (May 22, 1915), 75–76.

Aldington, Richard, "Modern Poetry and the Imagists." *The Egoist*, 1 (June 1, 1914), 201–3.

———, "The Imagists." *Bruno Chap Books*, II, Special Series No. 5 (1915), 69–76.

Baudelaire, Charles, *Oeuvres* (Texte établi et annoté par Y.-G. Le Dantec). Paris: La Pléiade, 1932, 1935. 2 vols.

Bergson, Henri Louis, *The Creative Mind: A Study in Metaphysics*, trans. by Mabelle L. Andison. New York: Philosophical Library, Inc., 1946.

———, *Laughter: An Essay on the Meaning of the Comic*, trans. by Cloudesley Brereton and Fred Rothwell. New York: The Macmillan Company, 1911.

Brace, Marjorie, "Worshipping Solid Objects: The Pagan World of Virginia Woolf." In Kerker Quinn and Charles Shattuck, eds., *Accent Anthology*, 489–95. New York: Harcourt, Brace & World, Inc., 1946.

Camus, Albert, *Le Mythe de Sisyphe*. Paris: Gallimard, 1942.

———, *The Myth of Sisyphus and Other Essays*, trans. by Justin O'Brien. New York: Alfred A. Knopf, Inc., 1961.

Coffman, Stanley K., *Imagism: A Chapter for the History of Modern Poetry*. Norman, Oklahoma: University of Oklahoma Press, 1951.

Dewey, John, *Art as Experience*. New York: G. P. Putnam's Sons, 1958.

Eliot, T. S., *Selected Essays, 1917–1932*. New York: Harcourt, Brace & World, Inc., 1932.

Firkins, O. W., "The New Movement in Poetry." *The Nation*, 101 (October 14, 1915), 458–61.

Fletcher, John Gould, "The Orient and Contemporary Poetry." In Arthur E. Christy, ed., *The Asian Legacy and American Life*, 145–74. New York: The John Day Company, Inc., 1945.

Flint, F. S., "The History of Imagism." *The Egoist*, 2 (May 1, 1915), 70–71.

———, "Imagisme." *Poetry*, 1 (March, 1913), 199.

———, "Presentation: Notes on the Art of Writing: on the Artfulness of Some Writers; and on the Artlessness of Others." *The Chap Book*, 2 (March, 1920), 17–24.

Ford, Ford Madox, "On Impressionism." *Poetry and Drama*, 5 (June, 1914), 167–75.

———, Techniques." *The Southern Review*, 1 (July, 1935), 20–35.

———, *The Critical Attitude*. London: Gerald Duckworth and Co., Ltd., 1914.

Gautier, Théophile, *Émaux et Camées*. Paris: Libraire Hachette, 1927.

Gourmont, Rémy de, *Decadence and Other Essays on the Culture of Ideas*, trans. by William Aspenwall Bradley. New York: Harcourt, Brace & Company, 1921.

Hughes, Glenn, *Imagism and the Imagists: A Study in Modern Poetry*. Stanford, California: Stanford University Press, 1931.

Hulme, T. E., *Speculations: Essays on Humanism and the Philosophy of Art*, Herbert Read, ed. London: Routledge and Kegan Paul, Ltd., 1949.

———, *Further Speculations*, Sam Hynes, ed. Minneapolis: The University of Minnesota Press, 1955.

Keats, John, *The Letters of John Keats, 1814–1821*, Hyder E. Rollins, ed. Cambridge, Massachusetts: Harvard University Press, 1950. 2 vols.

Lipman, Matthew, "The Physical Thing in Aesthetic Experience." *Journal of Aesthetics and Art Criticism*, 15 (September, 1956), 36–46.

Lowell, Amy, "A Consideration of Modern Poetry." *The North American Review*, 205 (January, 1917), 103–17.

———, *Tendencies in Modern American Poetry*. New York: The Macmillan Company, 1917.

———, "The New Manner in Modern Poetry." *The New Republic*, 6 (March 4, 1916), 124–25.

Mallarmé, Stéphane, *Oeuvres Complètes*. Paris: Gallimard, 1945.

———, *Propos sur la Poésie*, recueillis et présentés par Henri Mondor. Monaco: Éditions du Rocher, 1953.

Marcel, Gabriel, *The Philosophy of Existentialism*, trans. by Manya Harari. New York: The Citadel Press, 1961.

Maritain, Jacques, *Creative Intuition in Art and Poetry*. Bollingen Series, XXXV. New York: Pantheon Books, 1953.

Miner, Earl, *The Japanese Tradition in British and American Literature*. Princeton, New Jersey: Princeton University Press, 1958.

Nietzsche, Friedrich, *Gesammelte Werke*. Munchen: Musarion Verlag, 1920–1929. 23 vols.

Picard, Max, *Le Monde du Silence*, trans. by J. J. Anstett. Paris: Presses Universitaires de France, 1954.

Pound, Ezra, *ABC of Reading*. Norfolk, Connecticut: New Directions, 1934.

———, "A Few Don'ts by an Imagiste." *Poetry*, 1 (March, 1913) 200–201.

———, *Instigations of Ezra Pound, Together with an Essay on the Chinese Written Character, by Ernest Fenollosa*. New York: Boni & Liveright, 1920.

———, *Literary Essays of Ezra Pound*, T. S. Eliot, ed. Norfolk, Connecticut: New Directions, 1954.

———, *Pavannes and Divisions*. New York: Harcourt, Brace & Co., 1918.

———, *Personae: Collected Shorter Poems of Ezra Pound*. London: Faber and Faber, Ltd., 1952.

———, "Prologomena." *The Poetry Review*, 1 (February, 1912), 72–76.

———, "The Book of the Month." *The Poetry Review*, 1 (March, 1912), 133.

———, *The Letters of Ezra Pound 1907–41*, D. D. Paige, ed. New York: Harcourt, Brace & World, Inc., 1950.

———, "Vorticism," *The Fortnightly Review*, N.S. 97 (September 1, 1914), 461–71.

Ransom, John Crowe, *The World's Body*. New York: Charles Scribner's Sons, 1938.

Rodin, Auguste, *On Art and Artists*, trans. by Mrs. Romilly Fedden, from *L'art; entretiens réunis par Paul Gsell*. New York: Philosophical Library, 1957.

Some Imagist Poets: An Anthology. Boston: Houghton Mifflin Company, 1915.

Some Imagist Poets, 1916: An Annual Anthology. Boston: Houghton Mifflin Company, 1916.

Some Imagist Poets, 1917: An Annual Anthology. Boston: Houghton Mifflin Company, 1917.

Stevens, Wallace, *The Collected Poems of Wallace Stevens*. New York: Alfred A. Knopf, Inc., 1957.

———, *The Necessary Angel: Essays on Reality and the Imagination*. New York: Alfred A. Knopf, Inc., 1951.

Taupin, René, *L'Influence du Symbolisme Français sur la Poésie*

Américaine (de 1919 à 1920). Paris: Librairie Ancienne Honore Champion, 1929.

Thérive, André, *Le Parnasse*. Paris: Les Oeuvres représentatives, 1929.

Valéry, Paul, *Oeuvres*, Jean Hytier, ed. Paris: Librairie Gallimard, 1957. 2 vols.

Whitman, Walt, *Complete Prose Works*. New York: Mitchell Kennerley, 1891.

Wordsworth, William, *Prose Works*, rev. Alexander B. Grosart. New York: AMA Press, Inc., 1967. 3 vols.

Yasuda, Kenneth, *The Japanese Haiku: Its Essential Nature, History, and Possibilities in English, with Selected Examples*. Rutland, Vt.: Charles E. Tuttle Company, 1957.

Zukofsky, Louis, ed., *An "Objectivists" Anthology*. Le Beausset, France: To. Publishers, 1932.

II. WILLIAM CARLOS WILLIAMS

A. By Williams

"An Approach to the Poem." In *English Institute Essays* (1947), 50–75. New York: Columbia University Press, 1948.

Autobiography of William Carlos Williams, The. New York: Random House, Inc., 1951.

Collected Earlier Poems of William Carlos Williams, The. New York: New Directions, 1951.

Collected Later Poems of William Carlos Williams, The. New York: New Directions, 1950.

"Comment." *Contact,* 1 (May, 1932), 109–10.

"How to Write." *New Directions in Prose and Poetry,* I (1936), [57–60].

I Wanted to Write a Poem: The Autobiography of the Works of a Poet, reported and edited by Edith Heal. Boston: The Beacon Press, Inc., 1958.

In the American Grain. New York: New Directions, 1956.

Kora in Hell. Improvisations. San Francisco: City Lights Books, 1967.

"Notes from a Talk on Poetry." *Poetry,* 14 (July, 1919), 211–16.

Paterson, Books One-Four. New York: New Directions, 1951.

Paterson, Book Five. New York: New Directions, 1958.

Pictures from Breughel and Other Poems. New York: New Directions, 1962.

Selected Essays of William Carlos Williams. New York: Random House, Inc., 1954.

Selected Letters of William Carlos Williams, The. New York: McDowell, Obolensky, Inc., 1957.

The Tempers. London: E. Mathews, 1913.

"Tribute to Neruda the poet collector of seashells." *Rutgers Review,* 2 (Spring, 1967), 23–25.

B. About Williams

Brinnin, John W., *William Carlos Williams.* University of Minnesota Pamphlets on American Writers No. 24. Minneapolis: The University of Minnesota Press, 1963.

Burke, Kenneth, "The Methods of William Carlos Williams." *The Dial,* 82 (February, 1927), 94–98.

Calhoun, Richard J., " 'No Ideas but in Things': William Carlos Williams in the Twenties." In Richard E. Langford and

William E. Taylor, eds., *The Twenties, Poetry and Prose: Twenty Critical Essays*, 28–35. De Land, Florida: Everett Edwards, 1966.

Corman, Cid, "Double-Take: Another Response." *Folio*, 25 (Winter, 1960), 29–30.

Edelstein, Sanford, "William Carlos Williams: Essential Speech." *Perspective*, 6 (Winter, 1953), 224–28.

Engel, Bernard F., "A Democratic Vista of Religion." *Georgia Review*, 20 (Spring, 1966), 84–89. (Marianne Moore, William Carlos Williams, Wallace Stevens.)

————, "The Verse Line of Dr. Williams: A Fact of the Thing Itself." *Papers of the Michigan Academy of Science, Arts, and Letters, 46* (1960 meeting, published 1961), 665–70.

Guimond, James, *The Art of William Carlos Williams, A Discovery and Possession of America*. Urbana: The University of Illinois Press, 1969.

Hartung, Charles V., "A Poetry of Experience." *University of Kansas City Review*, 25 (Autumn, 1958), 65–69.

Heal, Elizabeth, "A Poet's Integrity: Letters from William Carlos Williams." *Literary Review*, 9 (Autumn, 1965), 115–19.

Jarrell, Randall, "An Introduction to the Selected Poems of William Carlos Williams." In his *Poetry and the Age*, 237–49. New York: Alfred A. Knopf, Inc., 1953.

————, "The Poet and his Public." *Partisan Review*, 13 (September–October, 1946), 488–99.

————, "To Measure Is All We Know." *Poetry*, 94 (May, 1959), 127–32.

————, "With the Bare Hands." *Poetry*, 80 (August, 1952), 276–90.

Koch, Vivienne, *William Carlos Williams*. New York: New Directions, 1950.

Koehler, G. Stanley, "A Gathering for William Carlos Williams." *Massachusetts Review*, 3 (Winter, 1962), 277–344. Contains contributions by Clinton J. Atkinson ("In Search of Theatre," 331–36), Carlos Baker ("A Complaint of Mutability," a poem for William Carlos Williams, 300), Cid Corman (*"The Farmers' Daughters*: A True Story About People," 319–24), H. E. F. Donohue ("An Occasion for Tremendous Music," 338–44), Raymond A. Kennedy (" 'Let's to Music, Hubert! ' : An Impertinent Piece," 336–38), Hugh Kenner ("The Drama of Utterance," 328–30), David Leviten ("I See," a poem for William Carlos Williams, 300), Mary Ellen Solt ("William Carlos Williams: Idiom and Structure," 304–18), John C. Thirlwall ("Four Unpublished Letters by William Carlos Williams," 292–96), Gael Turnbull ("A Visit to WCW; September, 1958," from his diary, 297–300), Louis Zukofsky ("An Old Note on WCW," 301–2); with poems, letters, fiction, and pages from a dramatic fragment of William Carlos Williams, and "Notes for a Gathering" by the editor.

Miller, J. Hillis, *William Carlos Williams: A Collection of Critical Essays.* Englewood Cliffs, New Jersey: Prentice-Hall, 1966. (Reprinted essays; includes Ezra Pound's "Dr. Williams' Position," 27–36; Marianne Moore's "Three Essays on Williams," 37–46; Kenneth Burke's "William Carlos Williams: Two Judgments," 47–61; Wallace Stevens' "William Carlos Williams," 63–65; Yvor Winters' "The Poetry of Feeling," 66–69; Louis L. Martz's "The Unicorn in *Paterson*: William Carlos Williams," 70–87; Ray Harvey Pearce's "Williams and the 'New Mode,'" 93–106; Sister M. Bernetta Quinn's "On *Paterson*, Book One," 107–20; Denis Donoghue's "For a Redeeming Language," 121–31; Karl Shapiro's "Study of 'Philomela Andronica'," 149–51; Robert Lowell's "William Carlos Williams," 153–59; Robert Creeley's "A Character to Love," 160–63; and Thomas Gunn's "William Carlos Williams," 171–73.)

———, *Poets of Reality: Six Twentieth-Century Writers.* Cambridge: Harvard University Press, 1966. (Conrad, Yeats, Eliot, Thomas, Stevens, William Carlos Williams.)

Morgan, Frederick, "William Carlos Williams: Imagery, Rhythm, Form." *Sewanee Review,* 55 (Summer, 1947), 675–91.

Myers, Neil, "Sentimentalism in the Early Poetry of William Carlos Williams." *American Literature,* 37 (January, 1966), 458–70.

———, "William Carlos Williams' *Spring and All.*" *Modern Language Quarterly,* 26 (June, 1965), 285–301.

Paul, Sherman, *The Music of Survival. A Biography of a Poem by William Carlos Williams.* Urbana: The University of Illinois Press, 1969.

Pearce, Roy Harvey, "The Poet as Person." *Yale Review,* 41 (Spring, 1952), 421–40.

Pearson, Norman Holmes, "Williams, New Jersey." *The Literary Review,* 1 (Autumn, 1957), 29–36.

Peterson, Walter Scott, *An Approach to Paterson.* New Haven: Yale University Press, 1967.

Quinn, Sister M. Bernetta, O.S.F., "William Carlos Williams: A Testament of Perpetual Change." In her *The Metamorphic Tradition of Modern Poetry. Essays on the Work of Ezra Pound, Wallace Stevens, William Carlos Williams, T. S. Eliot, Hart Crane, Randall Jarrell, and William Butler Yeats,* 89–129. New Brunswick, New Jersey: Rutgers University Press, 1955.

Solt, Mary Ellen, "Williams: Poems in the American Idiom." *Folio,* 25 (Winter, 1960), 3–28.

Stevens, Wallace, "Williams (Preface to *Collected Poems, 1921–1931*)," 254–57; "Rubbings of Reality," 257–59. In *Opus Posthumus*. New York: Alfred A. Knopf, Inc., 1957.

Sutton, Walter, "A Visit with William Carlos Williams." *Minnesota Review*, 1 (Winter, 1961), 209–324.

Wagner, Linda, "A Bunch of Marigolds." *Kenyon Review*, 29 (January, 1967), 86–102. (Williams' later poetry.)

———, "A Decade of Discovery, 1953–1963: Checklist of Criticism, William Carlos Williams' Poetry." *Twentieth Century Literature*, 10 (January, 1965), 166–69.

———, "The Last Poems of William Carlos Williams." *Criticism*, 6 (Fall, 1964), 361–78.

———, *The Poems of William Carlos Williams, A Critical Study*. Middletown, Connecticut: Wesleyan University Press, 1964.

———, "William Carlos Williams: Classic American Poet." *Renascence*, 16 (Spring, 1964), 115–25.

Wallace, Emily Mitchell, *A Bibliography of William Carlos Williams*. Middletown, Connecticut: Wesleyan University Press, 1969.

Weatherhead, A. Kingsley, "William Carlos Williams: Poetic Invention and the World Beyond." *Journal of English Literary History*, 32 (March, 1965), 126–38.

———, "William Carlos Williams: Prose, Form, and Measure." *English Literary History*, 33 (March, 1966), 118–31.

Wilson, T. C., "The Animate Touch." *Briarcliff Quarterly*, 3 (October, 1946), 195–98.

Winters, Yvor, "Primitivism and Decadence: A Study of American Experimental Poetry." In his *In Defense of Reason*, 3–15. Denver, Colorado: University of Denver Press, 1943. (This essay contains scattered discussions of individual poems.)

Zukofsky, Louis, "A Note on the Work of William Carlos Williams." *Briarcliff Quarterly*, 3 (October, 1946), 198–201.

III. FRANCIS PONGE

A. By Ponge:

"Cher Calet." *Le Figaro littéraire,* 11 (juillet–décembre, 1956), 1, 10.
Dix Courts sur la méthode. Paris: Pierre Seghers, 1946.
La Seine. Images de Maurice Blanc. Lausanne: La Guilde du livre, 1950.
Le Carnet du bois de pins. Lausanne: Mermod, 1947.
Le Grand Recueil. Paris: Gallimard, 1961. 3 vols.: I. *Lyres;* II. *Méthodes;* III. *Pièces.*
Le Parti pris des choses. Paris: Gallimard, 1942.
Le Savon. Paris: Gallimard, 1967.
Nouveau Recueil. Paris: Gallimard, 1967.
Pour un Malherbe. Paris: Gallimard, 1965.
Proêmes. Paris: Gallimard, 1948.
Tome premier. Paris: Gallimard, 1965. (Contains "Douze petits écrits," "La Rage de l'expression," "Le Peintre a l'étude."
Translations:
Hoy, Peter, "A Note on Francis Ponge." *Luciad* (March, 1966), 32, Followed by five translations of prose fragments: "Introduction to the Pebble" (extracts, 1933), 33; "Pastoral Symphony" (1937), 34; "The Notebook of the Pine Grove" (extract: August 20, 1960), 34–35; "Fire" (1942), 35; "Rain" (1942), 36.
Macbeth, George, "A Note on Ponge." *Stand* (1965), 64. Followed by an English adaptation of *La Guêpe: The Wasp-Woman,* 65–75.
"Prose Sketches," trans. by Lane Dunlop. *Art and Literature,* 12 (Spring, 1967), 225–52.
"Soap," trans. by Lane Dunlop. "The Peasant House," "The Parabolic Heater," "The Shape of the World," "The Asparagus-fern," trans. by Sarah Plimpton. *The Paris Review,* 43 (Summer, 1968), 112–39.
"The End of Autumn," "Rum of Ferns," "The Oyster," trans. by Lane Dunlop. *Prairie Schooner,* 41 (Winter, 1967), 421–22.
The Penguin Book of French Verse: The Twentieth Century, trans. by Anthony Hartley, ed. Middlesex, Great Britain: Penguin Books, Ltd., 1959. (Contains translations of "Le Tronc d'arbre," "Les Trois Boutiques," "L'Huître," "Le Papillon," "Notes pour un coquillage.")
"The Season's Cycle," "The Mollusc," "The Butterfly," "Moss," "Seashores," "On Water," (from *Le Parti pris des choses*), trans. by Lane Dunlop. *Chelsea, 22/23* (June, 1968), 81–85.

"Francis Ponge's 'The Spider,'" trans. by Mark J. Temmer. *Prairie Schooner*, 40 (Spring, 1966), 44–48.

"The Sun of the Abyss," trans. by Lane Dunlop. *Harper's Bazaar*, 100 (January, 1967), 104–5, 148.

B. *About Ponge:*

Alyn, Marc, "Francis Ponge: *Le Grand Recueil.*" *La Table ronde*, 170 (mars, 1962), 110–11.

Arseguel, Gérard, "Pour un Malherbe ou le temps de la parole." *Cahiers du Sud*, 59 (février–mars, 1965), 105–9.

Bigongiari, Piero, "Enfin Ponge vint." *Paragone*, 16 (ottobre, 1965), 151–59.

———, "Intervista con Ponge." *L'Approdo Letterario*, 7 (aprile-septembre, 1961), 178–82.

———, "Le Parti pris de Ponge." *La Nouvelle revue française*, 4 (septembre, 1956), 417–21.

———, "Un autre Ponge." *Tel Quel* (hiver, 1962), 29–33.

Bordier, Roger, "Francis Ponge: l'objet." *Les Nouvelles littéraires*, 41 (25 juillet 1963), 8.

———, "Un complot contre l'homme." *Les Nouvelles littéraires*, 40 (30 août 1962), 1.

Bosquet, Alain, "Francis Ponge, poète de l'objet." *Le Monde*, 692 (18–24 janvier 1962), 10.

———, "Rêverie sur le premier Ponge." *La Nouvelle nouvelle revue française*, 14 (1 juillet 1966), 98–106.

Braque, Georges, "Parti du plus bas." *La Nouvelle revue française*, 4 (septembre, 1956), 385.

Burgart, Jean-Pierre, "Sur le point de parler." *Mercure de France*, 339 (juillet, 1960), 427–33.

Camus, Albert, "Lettre au sujet du 'Parti pris,'" *La Nouvelle revue française*, 4 (septembre, 1956), 386–92.

Carner, José, "Francis Ponge et les choses." *La Nouvelle revue française*, 4 (septembre, 1956), 409–12.

———, "Francis Ponge y las cosas." *Sur*, 230 (septiembre–octubre, 1954), 71–73.

Carrouges, Michel, "La rage de l'expression. L'Araignée par Francis Ponge." *Monde nouveau-paru*, 9, No. 66 (sommaire, 1953), 99–102.

Christoff, Bernard, "La notion de limite." *Revue de belles-lettres*, 90 (février–mars, 1942), 4.

Clancier, G. E., "Un poète dans tous ses états." *Cahiers du Sud*, 50 (juillet-août, 1963), 283–89.

De Solier, Rene, "Douze petits écrites, ou l'emulsion du langage." *Synthèses*, 11 (avríl/mai–juillet, 1956), 459–77.

Deguy, Michel, "Ponge-Pilate." *Critique*, 22 (novembre, 1966) 923–29.

Denat, Antoine, "Après le grand Recueil ou le Ponge de l'objet.' *Synthèses*, 18 (mai, 1963), 76–87.

———, "Francis Ponge and the New Problem of the *Epos*." *University of Queensland Papers*, 1 (1963), 35–41.

———, "Towards an Ontology of the Poem (from Valéry to Ponge)." *Journal of the Australasian Universities Language and Literature Association*, 6 (May, 1957), 14–19.

Douthat, Blossom Margaret, "Francis Ponge's Untenable Goat." *Yale French Studies*, 21 (Spring–Summer, 1958), 172–81.

———, "Le Parti pris des *choses?*" *French Studies*, 13 (January, 1959), 39–51.

Du Bouchet, A., "Francis Ponge." *Critique*, 45 (February, 1951), 182–83.

Duché, Jean, "Francis Ponge et le langage." *Synthèses*, 5 (juillet, 1950), 224–28.

Étiemble, "Pour Francis Ponge." *Les Temps modernes*, 5 (mai, 1950), 2087–92.

Garelli, Jacques, "De la définition du dictionnaire au dévoilement poétique: L'enterprise de Ponge." In his *La gravitation poétique*, 72–79. Paris: Mercure de France, 1966.

Grenier, Jean, "Présentation de Francis Ponge." *La Nouvelle revue française*, 4 (septembre, 1956), 393–95.

Gros, Leon, "Francis Ponge ou la rhétorique humanisée." *Cahiers du Sud*, 25 (1947), 1015–19.

Hahn, Otto, "Les ambiguités de Ponge." *Les Temps modernes*, 17 (mars, 1962), 1362–66.

Jaccottet, Philippe, "Remarques sur 'Le soleil.'" *La Nouvelle revue française*, 4 (septembre, 1956), 396–405.

Kréa, Henri, "Enfin sorti de la clandestinité: Francis Ponge à al portée de tous." *Arts*, 851 (10–16 janvier 1962), 3.

Krolow, Karl, "Sprechen gegen die Worte." *Neue Deutsche hefte*, 74 (September, 1960), 548–50.

Loy, J. Robert, " 'Things' in Recent French Literature." *Publications of the Modern Language Association*, 71 (March, 1956), 27–41.

Magny, Claude-Edmonde, "F.P. ou l'homme heureux." *Poésie*, 46 (juin–juillet, 1946), 62–68.

Marzi, Carla, "Francis Ponge." *L'Approdo Letterario*, 11 (gennaio–marzo, 1965), 106–10.

Mauriac, Claude, "Malherbe, comme la crevette." *L'Express*, 713 (15–21 février 1965), 54–55.

Micha, René, "Sur Francis Ponge, poète vêtu comme un arbre." *Revue de Suisse*, 2 (30 juin–31 juillet 1952), 49–56.

Miller, Betty, "Francis Ponge and the Creative Method." *Horizon*, 16 (September, 1947), 214–20.

———, "Personne a l'Horizon." *La Nouvelle revue française*, 4 (septembre, 1956), 413–16.

Mounin, Georges, "L'Anti-Pascal, ou la poésie et les vacances, Francis Ponge." *Critique*, 5 (juin, 1949), 493–500.

Nadal, Octave, "Dans les secrets d'une création poétique." *Le Figaro littéraire*, 15 (11 juin 1960), 4.

———, "Une oeuvre en cours. . . ." In his *À mesure haute*, 277–80. Paris: Mercure de France, 1964.

Nimier, Roger, "Francis Ponge." In his *Journées de lectures*, 230–34. Paris: Gallimard, 1965.

Noulet, Emilie, "L'oeuvre poétique de Francis Ponge." In her *Alphabet critique, 1924–1964*, 226–32. Bruxelles: Presses Universitaires de Bruxelles, 1965.

———, "Ponge, Francis: La rage de l'expression." In her *Alphabet critique, 1924–1964*, 222–25. Bruxelles: Presses Universitaires de Bruxelles, 1965.

Onimus, Jean, "L'homme égaré: Notes sur le sentiment d'égarement dans la littérature actuelle." *Études*, 283 (décembre, 1954), 320–29.

Petit, Henri, "Ponge virtuose." *Les Nouvelles littéraires*, 40 (18 janvier 1962), 4–5.

Pieyre de Mandiargues, André, " 'Le Soleil' de Ponge." In his *Le Cadran lunaire*, 125–29. Paris: Robert Laffont, 1958.

———, "Le Feu et la pierre." *La Nouvelle revue française*, 4 (septembre, 1956), 406–8.

Plank, David G., "*Le Grand Recueil*: Francis Ponge's Optimistic Materialism." *Modern Language Quarterly*, 26 (June, 1965) 302–17.

"The Quest for a Major Poet," (no author given). *London Times Literary Supplement* (May 4, 1962), 313.

Recht, Roland, "La pomme de terre de Ponge." *Cahiers des saisons*, 34 (été, 1963), 478–80.

Richard, Jean-Pierre, "Francis Ponge." In his *Onze études sur la poésie moderne*, 161–81. Paris: Éditions du Seuil, 1964.

———, "Les Partis pris de Ponge." *La Nouvelle nouvelle revue française*, 12 (avril, 1964), 627–55.

Rolland de Renéville, A., "Sur un livre de Francis Ponge." *La Nef*, 4 (mai, 1947), 120–23.

Rousseaux, André, "Francis Ponge et la nature des choses." *Le Figaro littéraire*, 4 (9 avril 1949), 2.

Saillet, Maurice, "Le proête Ponge." *Mercure de France*, 306 (1 juin 1949), 305–13.

Sartre, Jean-Paul, *Situations*. Paris: Gallimard, 1947–1965, 7 vols. (See especially "L'Homme et les choses," I, 275–93.)

———, *La Nausée*. Paris: Gallimard, 1938.

———, *Nausea*, trans. by Lloyd Alexander. New York: New Directions [1949?].

———, "Sobre un libro de Francis Ponge: 'A favor de las cosas.' " *Sur*, 14 (mayo, 1945), 56–72.

Schneider, Pierre, "Francis Ponge, ou l'écriture grandeur nature." *Synthèses*, 8 (avril–juillet, 1953), 59–63.

———, "Introduction to the Works of Francis Ponge." *Transition Fifty*, 6 (1950), 68–74.

Sénard, Jean, "Francis Ponge, ambassadeur du monde muet." *Le Figaro littéraire*, 16 (23 décembre 1961), 3.

Simon, Pierre-Henri, "D'une nouvelle façon de regarder: Francis Ponge, Alain Robbe-Grillet, Philippe Sollers." In his *Diagnostic des lettres françaises contemporaines*, 295–302. Bruxelles: La Renaissance du livre, 1966.

Sollers, Philippe, "Francis Ponge, ou la raison à plus haut prix." *Mercure de France*, 339 (1 juillet 1960), 406–26.

Thibaudeau, Jean, "Les 'poésies' de Ponge." *Critique*, 31 (août–septembre, 1965), 752–62.

Torel, Jean, "Francis Ponge et la formulation globale." *Cahiers du Sud*, 40 (sommaire, 1953), 492–500.

———, "Francis Ponge et la morale de l'expression." *Critique*, 18 (juin, 1962), 481–94.

———, "*Le Parti pris des choses*, par Francis Ponge." Collection Métamorphosis, Gallimard. *Cahiers du Sud*, 31 (août–septembre, 1944), 99–103.

———, "Poème à Francis Ponge." *Cahiers du Sud*, 29–30 (sommaire, 1949), 477–84.

Vigée, Claude, "Metamorphoses of Modern Poetry." *Comparative Literature*, 7 (Spring, 1955), 97–120.

Walther, Elisabeth, *Francis Ponge: Eine ästhetische Analyse*. Köln: Kiepenheuer und Witsch, 1965.

Y.L., "The Poet's Virginity." *Dublin Magazine*, 23 (October–December, 1948), 39–47. (Valéry and Ponge.)

Zeltner-Neukomm, Gerda, "Un Poète de natures mortes." *La Nouvelle revue française*, 4 (septembre, 1956), 422–25.

IV. RAINER MARIA RILKE

A. By Rilke:

Briefe, herausgegeben vom Rilke-Archiv in Weimar; in Verbindung mit Ruth Sieber-Rilke besorgt durch Karl Altheim. 2 vols.: I, 1897 bis 1914; II, 1914 bis 1926. Wiesbaden: Insel-Verlag, 1950.

Briefe aus den Jahren 1902 bis 1906, herausgegeben von Ruth Sieber-Rilke und Carl Sieber. Leipzig: Insel-Verlag, 1930.

Briefe aus den Jahren 1906 bis 1907, herausgegeben von Ruth Sieber-Rilke und Carl Sieber. Leipzig: Insel-Verlag, 1930.

Briefe aus den Jahren 1907 bis 1914, herausgegeben von Ruth Sieber-Rilke und Carl Sieber. Leipzig: Insel-Verlag, 1933.

Briefe aus den Jahren 1914 bis 1921, herausgegeben von Ruth Sieber-Rilke und Carl Sieber. Leipzig: Insel-Verlag, 1937.

Briefe aus Muzot, 1921 bis 1926, herausgegeben von Ruth Sieber-Rilke und Carl Sieber. Leipzig: Insel-Verlag, 1935.

Briefwechsel mit Benvenuta, herausgegeben von Magda v. Hattingberg. Esslingen: Bechtle Verlag, 1954.

Bucher. Theater. Kunst, herausgegeben von Richard Mises. Vienna: Jahoda und Siegel Verlag, 1934.

"Erlebnis." In *Insel-Almanach auf das Jahr 1919,* 40–43. Leipzig: Insel-Verlag, 1919.

Rainer Maria Rilke — Lou Andreas-Salomé, Briefwechsel, herausgegeben von Ernst Pfeiffer. Zürich: Max Niehans Verlag, 1952.

Rainer Maria Rilke et Merline: Correspondance 1920–1926, rédaction par Dieter Bassermann. Zürich: Max Niehans Verlag, 1954.

Sämtliche Werke, herausgegeben vom Rilke-Archiv: in Verbindung mit Ruth Sieber-Rilke besorgt durch Karl Altheim. Wiesbaden: Insel-Verlag. I, 1955; II, 1956; III, 1959; IV, 1961.

"Uber den jungen Dichter." In *Insel-Almanach auf das Jahr 1939,* 33–40. Leipzig: Insel-Verlag, 1939.

"Ur-Geräusch." *Das Inselschiff,* 1 (Oktober, 1919), 14–20.

"Von der Landschaft." In *Insel-Almanach auf das Jahr 1933,* 40–46. Leipzig: Insel-Verlag, 1933.

Werke; Auswahl in Zwei Bänden: Prosa, herausgegeben von Fritz Adolf Hunich. Leipzig: Insel-Verlag, 1957.

Translations:

Duino Elegies, trans. by J. B. Leishman and Stephen Spender. New York: W. W. Norton & Company, Inc., 1939.

Letters of Rainer Maria Rilke, 1892–1910, trans. by Jane Bannard Greene and M. D. Herter Norton. New York: W. W. Norton & Company, Inc., 1945.

Letters of Rainer Maria Rilke, 1910–1926, Vol. II, trans. by Jane Bannard Greene and M. D. Herter Norton. New York: W. W. Norton & Company, Inc., 1948.

Letters to Benvenuta, trans. by Heinz Nordon. New York: Philosophical Library, Inc., 1951.

Letters to Merline, 1919–1922, trans. by Violet M. Macdonald. London: Methuen & Co., Ltd., 1951.

Letters to a Young Poet, rev. ed., trans. by M. D. Herter Norton. New York: W. W. Norton & Company, Inc., 1952.

New Poems, trans. by J. B. Leishman. New York: New Directions, 1964.

Poems 1906 to 1926, trans. by J. B. Leishman. New York: New Directions, 1957.

Rainer Maria Rilke: The Years in Switzerland. Letters trans. by N. K. Cruickshank from the German edition of 1936. London: The Hogarth Press, 1964.

Selected Works: Prose, Vol. I, trans. by G. Craig Houston. New York: New Directions, 1960.

Selected Works: Poetry, Vol. II, trans. by J. B. Leishman. London: The Hogarth Press, 1960.

Sonnets to Orpheus, trans. by M. D. Herter Norton. New York: W. W. Norton & Company, Inc., 1942.

The Letters of Rainer Maria Rilke and Princess Marie von Thurn und Taxis, trans. by Nora Wydenbruck. New York: New Directions, 1958.

The Life of the Virgin Mary, trans. by C. F. MacIntyre. Berkeley: University of California Press, 1947.

The Notebooks of Malte Laurids Briggs, trans. by M. D. Herter Norton. New York: W. W. Norton & Company, Inc., 1949.

Wartime Letters of Rainer Maria Rilke, 1914–1921, trans. by M. D. Herter Norton. New York: W. W. Norton & Company, Inc., 1940.

B. About Rilke:

Andelson, Robert V., "The Concept of Creativity in the Thought of Rilke and Berdyaev." *The Personalist*, 43 (Spring, 1962), 226–32.

Angelloz, J. F., *Rainer Maria Rilke: L'Évolution Spirituelle du Poète*. Paris: Paul Hartmann, 1936.

Basserman, Dieter, *Der andere Rilke: Gesammelte Schriften aus dem Nachlass*, herausgegeben von Hermann Mörchen. Bad Homburg: Gentner, 1961.

Belmore, Herbert W., and Heidi Heimann, " 'Behangen Wie ein Stier': Entgegnung und Berichtigung." *Publications of the English Goethe Society*, N. S. 33 (Papers read before the Society, 1962–1963), 1–9.

Bemól, Maurice, "Rilke et Valéry." In his *Variations sur Valéry*, II, 159–74. Paris: G. Nizet, 1959.

Berendt, Hans, *Rainer Maria Rilkes Neue Gedichte: Versuch einer Deutung*. Bonn: H. Bouvier und Co. Verlag, 1957.

Betz, Marice, *Rilke à Paris, et Les Cahiers de Malte Laurids Brigge*. Paris: Éditions Émile-Paul Frères, 1941.

Bollinow, Otto F., *Rilke*. Stuttgart: Kohlhammer, 1951.

Boney, Elaine E., "The Concept of Being in Rilke's *Elegien*." *Symposium*, 15 (Spring, 1961), 12–21.

——, "The Role of the Paradox in Rilke's 'Sonnette.' " *The South Central Bulletin*, 22 (Winter, 1962), 19–23.

Butler, E. M., *Rainer-Maria Rilke*. Cambridge: The University Press, 1941.

Cassirer-Soltnitz, Eva, *Die Sonnette an Orpheus*. Heidelberg: Koester, 1957.

Costa, John, "Aesthetics Behind the Poems of Charles Baudelaire and Rainer Maria Rilke on Autumn." *Culture*, 27 (September, 1966), 350–55.

David, Claude, "Rilke et l'expressionisme." *Études germaniques*, 16 (avril–juin, 1962), 144–57.

Dédéyan, Charles, *Rilke et la France*. Paris: Société d'Education et d'Enseignement Supérieur, 1961.

Deleu, K., "Eine unbekannte Trilogie in Rilkes Neuen Gedichten." *Studia Germanica*, I (1960), 189–220.

Despert, Jehan, *La pensée de Rainer-Maria Rilke à travers les grands thèmes de son oeuvre*. Bruxelles: Eds du Cercle d'études litteraires françaises, 1962.

Diez del Corral, Luis, "Rilkes Orpheus," trans. into German by Gustave Conradi. *Antaios*, 4 (July, 1962), 120–35.

Emde, Ursula, *Rilke und Rodin*. Marburg/Lahn: Verlag des Kunstgeschichtlichen Seminars, 1949.

Feise, Ernest, "Rilkes Weg zu den Dingen." *Monatshefte*, 28 (April, 1936), 151–56.

Fickert, Kurt J., "Form and Meaning in Rilke's Sonnets." *Kentucky Foreign Language Quarterly*, 10 (Second Quarter, 1963), 69–81.

Fulleborn, Ulrich, *Das Strukturproblem der späten Lyrik Rilkes: Voruntersuchungen zu einem historischen Rilke-Verständnis*. Heidelberg: Winter, 1960.

Graff, W. C., *Rainer Maria Rilke: Creative Anguish of a Modern*

Poet. Princeton, New Jersey: Princeton University Press, 1956.

Hagen, Hans-Wilhelm, *Rilkes Umarbeitungen, ein Betrag zur Psychologie seines Dichterischen Schaffens*. Leipzig: Hermann Eichblatt Verlag, 1931.

Hamburger, Kate, *Philosophie der Dichter: Novalis, Schiller, Rilke*. Stuttgart: Kohlhammer, 1966.

Hartman, Geoffrey H., "Rainer Maria Rilke." In his *The Unmediated Vision: An Interpretation of Wordsworth, Hopkins, Rilke, and Valéry*, 69–96. New Haven: Yale University Press, 1954.

Heerikhuizen, F. W. van, *Rainer Maria Rilke, His Life and Work*, trans. by Fernand G. Renier and Anne Cliff. London: Routledge and Kegan Paul, Ltd., 1951.

Heftrich, Eckhard, *Die Philosophie und Rilke*. Symposion; philosophische schriftenreihe, 9. Freiberg: K. Alber, 1962.

Hergershausen, Lore, "Sur quelques termes du vocabulaire des arts plastiques dans l'oeuvre de R. M. Rilke: Les reflets." *Études germaniques*, 17 (juillet–septembre, 1962), 281–89.

Holthusen, Hans Egon, *Rainer Maria Rilke: A Study of His Later Poetry*, trans. by J. P. Stern. New Haven: Yale University Press, 1952.

———, "Rilke und die Dichtung der Gegenwart." *Universitas*, 12 (November, 1957), 1157–70.

Holroyd, Stuart, *Emergence from Chaos*. London: Victor Gollancz, Ltd., 1957.

Houston, G. Craig, "Rilke und Rodin." In *German Studies, Presented to Professor H. G. Fiedler, by pupils, colleagues and friends on his seventy-fifth birthday, 28 April 1937*, 244–65. Oxford: The Clarendon Press, 1938.

Jaszi, Andrew O., "Names and Objects in Rilke's Poetry." *New Mexico Quarterly*, 25 (Spring, 1955), 73–81.

Kunisch, Hermann, *Rainer Maria Rilke und die Dinge*. Köln: Balduin Pick Verlag, 1946.

Lang, Renée, "Rilke and his French Contemporaries." *Comparative Literature*, 10 (Spring, 1958), 136–43.

Legrand, Jacques, "Les avatars d'un Sonnet à Orphée." *Die neueren Sprachen*, 14 (November, 1965), 531–36.

Lettau, Reinhard, "Rilkes Zyklus 'Die Parke.'" *Monatshefte*, 51 (April–Mai, 1959), 169–72.

Mandel, Siegfried, "Notes on the Translations of Rilke's 'Archaic Torso of Apollo.'" *Criticism*, 6 (Winter, 1964), 17–32.

———, *Rainer Maria Rilke: The Poetic Instinct*. Carbondale: Southern Illinois University Press, 1965.

Mason, Eudo C., *Lebenshaltung und Symbolik bei Rainer Maria Rilke*. Weimar: H. Böhlau, 1939.

———, *Rainer Maria Rilke: Sein Leben und sein Werk*. Göttingen: Vandenhoeck und Ruprecht, 1964.

———, *Rilke, Europe, and the English-Speaking World*. Cambridge: The University Press, 1961.

———, "Rilke's Experience of Inspiration and his Conception of 'Ordnen.'" *Forum for Modern Language Studies*, 2 (April, 1966), 335–46. University of Saint Andrews, Scotland.

McGlashen, L., "Rilke's *Neue Gedichte*." *German Life and Letters*, 12 (January, 1959), 81–101.

Mühlher, Robert, "Rilke und Cézanne: Eine Studie über die künstlerische Methode des 'Einsehens.'" *Osterreich in Geschichte und Literatur*, 10 (Jänner–Februar, 1966), 35–47.

Müller, Joachim, "Atmen, du unsichtbares Gedicht!" *Wirkendes Wort*, 9 (September–Oktober, 1959), 286–91.

Müller, Paul E., "Rilkes Stellung zur Sprache: Interpretation von Sonett XV unter Zuhilfenahme der 9. Duinser Elegie." *Der Deutschunterricht*, 10 (September–Oktober, 1958), 39–44.

Obermüller, Paul, Herbert Steiner, and Ernst Zinn, eds., *Katalog der Rilke-Sammlung Richard von Mises*, bearbeitet und herausgegeben von Paul Obermüller und Herbert Steiner unter Mitarbeit von Ernst Zinn. Frankfurt am Main: Insel-Verlag, 1966.

Oliver, Kenneth, "Rainer Maria Rilke's Basic Concept of Literary Art." *Monatshefte*, 40 (November, 1948), 382–90.

Parry, Idris, "Unicorn and Narcissus: A Study of Three of Rilke's 'Sonnette an Orpheus.'" *Modern Language Review*, 54 (July, 1959), 378–83.

Peters, H. F., *Rainer Maria Rilke: Masks and the Man*. Seattle: University of Washington Press, 1960.

Quasha, George, "Test of Translation VI: Rilke's Third Duino Elegy." *Caterpillar*, I (October, 1967), 200–208. (A new translation transposed into stanzas and lines of varied lengths.)

Rickman, H. P., "Poetry and the Ephemeral: Rilke's and Eliot's Conception of the Poet's Task." *German Life and Letters*, 12 (April, 1959), 174–85.

Ritzer, Walter, *Rainer Maria Rilke Bibliographie*. Wien: Verlag O. Kerry, 1951.

Robinet de Cléry, Adrien, *Rainer-Maria Rilke: Sa vie, son oeuvre, sa pensée*. Paris: Presses Universitaires de France, 1958.

Rohm, Karl, ed., *Jahresgabe: Josef Weinheber-Gesellschaft*. Wien: Weinheber-Gesellschaft, 1960. (Contains "Aus den Nachdichtungen von Rainer Maria Rilkes Zyklus 'Les Roses,'" 6011.)

Rose, William, and G. Craig Houston, eds., *Rainer Maria Rilke: Aspects of his Mind and Poetry*. London: Sidgwick & Jackson, Ltd., 1938.

Schlötermann, Heinz, *Rainer Maria Rilke: Versuch einer Wesens-deutung*. München: Reinhardt, 1966.

Shaw, Priscilla Washburn, *Rilke, Valéry and Yeats: The Domain of the Self*. New Brunswick, New Jersey: Rutgers University Press, 1964.

Spitzer, Leo, "Zum Rilke-Sonnett 'Atmen, du unsichtbares Gedicht!'" *Wirkendes Wort*, 10 (Januar-Februar, 1959), 52.

Steiner, Jakob, *Rilkes "Duineser Elegien."* Bern: Francke, 1962.

Stewart, Corbet, "Rilke's Cycle 'Die Parke,'" *Modern Language Review*, 61 (April, 1966), 238–39.

Storck, Joachim W., "Wort-Kerne und Dinge: Rilke und die Krise der Sprache. Zu den 'Gedichten 1906 bis 1926.'" *Akzente*, 4 (August, 1957), 346–58.

Strauss, Walter A., "The Reconciliation of Opposites in Orphic Poetry: Rilke and Mallarmé." *The Centennial Review*, 10 (Spring, 1966), 214–36.

Uyttersprot, H., "R. H. Rilkes 'Die Gazelle.'" *Der Deutschunterlicht*, 14 (July, 1962), 20–29.

Weigand, Herman J., "Rilkes 'Archaischer Torso Apollos.'" *Monatshefte*, 51 (Februar, 1959), 49–62.

——, "Rilkes 'Romische Sarkophage.'" In *Dichtung und Deutung: Gedachtnisschrift für Hans M. Wolff*, K. S. Guthoke, ed., 153–62. Bern: Francke, 1961.

Wolfe, Ernest M., "Rilke's 'L'Ange du Méridien'; A Thematic Analysis." *Publications of the Modern Language Society*, 80 (March, 1965), 9–18.

Wood, Frank, "Rilke and the Time Factor." *Germanic Review*, 14 (October, 1929), 183–91.

——, *The Ring of Forms*. Minneapolis: The University of Minnesota Press, 1958.

V. PABLO NERUDA

A. By Neruda:

A la memoria de Ricardo Fonseca, 21 julio 1949–1951. Editorial de homenaje: Santiago de Chile, n.d.

Cantos ceremoniales. Buenos Aires: Editorial Losada, 1961.

Cien sonetos de amor. Buenos Aires: Editorial Losada, 1960.

Diez odas para diez grabados de Roser Bru. Barcelona: Ediciones el laberinth, 1965.

El habitante y su esperanza. El hondero entusiasta. Tentativa del hombre infinito. Anillos. Buenos Aires: Editorial Losada, 1957.

Estravagario. Buenos Aires: Editorial Losada, 1958.

Fulgor y muerte de Joaquín Murieta, bandido chileno injusticiado en California el 23 de julio de 1853. Santiago de Chile: Zig-Zag, 1966.

La barcarola. Buenos Aires: Editorial Losada, 1967.

La insepulta de Paita. Elegía dedicada a la memoria de Manuela Sáenz, amante de Simón Bolívar. Grabados en madera por Luis Seoane. Buenos Aires: Editorial Losada, 1962.

Las piedras de Chile. Buenos Aires: Editorial Losada, 1960.

Las uvas y el viento. Santiago de Chile: Nascimento, 1954.

Memorial de Isla Negra: Vol. I, *Donde nace la lluvia*; Vol. II, *La luna en el laberinto*; Vol. III, *El fuego cruel*; Vol. IV, *El cazador de raíces*; Vol. V, *Sonata crítica.* Buenos Aires: Editorial Losada, 1964.

Navegaciones y regresos. Buenos Aires: Editorial Losada, 1959.

Obras completas. Buenos Aires: Editorial Losada, 1965.

Plenos poderes. Buenos Aires: Editorial Losada, 1962.

Tercer libro de las odas. Buenos Aires: Editorial Losada, 1957.

Una casa en la arena. Barcelona: Lumen, 1966.

Viajes. Santiago de Chile: Nascimento, 1955. (Includes "Viaje al corazón de Quevedo" and "Viaje por las costas del mundo.")

Translations:

Bestiary. Bestiario; a poem, trans. by Elsa Neuberger. New York: Harcourt, Brace & World, Inc., 1965.

Early Poems, The, trans. by Davis Ossman and Carlos B. Hagen. New York: New Rivers Press, 1969.

Elementary Odes of Pablo Neruda, The, trans. by Carlos Lozano. New York: Las Americas Publishing Company, 1961.

Heights of Macchu Picchu, The, trans. by Nathaniel Tarn. New York: Farrar, Straus & Giroux, Inc., 1967.

Let the Rail Splitter Awake and Other Poems, by various translators. New York: Masses & Mainstream, Inc., 1951.

Logue, Christopher, *The Man Who Told His Love; 20 Poems*

Based on Pablo Neruda's "Los cantos d'amores." North-wood, Middlesex: Scorpion Press, 1958.

New Decade: Poems 1958–1967. Ben Belitt, ed. New York: Grove Press, Inc., 1969.

Residence on Earth and Other Poems, trans. by Angel Flores. New York: New Directions, 1946.

Selected Poems of Pablo Neruda, trans. by Ben Belitt. New York: Grove Press, Inc., 1961.

Twenty Poems, trans. by James Wright and Robert Bly. Madison, Minnesota: The Sixties Press, 1967.

We Are Many, trans. by Alastair Reid. London: Cape Goliard Press, Ltd., 1967.

B. About Neruda:

Aguirre, Margarita, *Genio y figura de Pablo Neruda.* Buenos Aires: Editorial Universitaria de Buenos Aires, 1964.

Alazraki, Jaime, *Poética y poesía de Pablo Neruda.* New York: Las Americas Publishing Company, 1965.

Alberti, Rafael, "De mon amitié avec Pablo Neruda." *Europe,* 42 (mars–avril, 1964), 71–75.

Alegría, Fernando, "Pablo Neruda: Two Worlds in Conflict." *Berkeley Review,* 1 (Spring, 1957), 27–33.

Alonso, Amado, *Poesía y estilo de Pablo Neruda.* Buenos Aires: Editorial sudamericana, 1966.

Augier, Angel, Rafaela Chacón, José L. Balde, Nicolás Guillén, Jan Marinello, Mirta Aguirre, y E. Labrador Ruíz, *Homenaje cubano a Pablo Neruda.* La Habana: Palacio Municipal, 1948.

Bellini, Guiseppe, "La Francia nell'Opera di Pablo Neruda." *Studi di letteratura, storia e filosofia in onore di Bruno Revel.* Biblioteca dell' "Archivum Romanicum," Ser. I, Vol. 74, 101–12. Firenze: L. S. Olschki, 1965.

Bly, Robert, "A Conversation about Hernandez." *The Sixties,* 9 (Spring, 1967), 4–6. (Interview with Neruda.)

———, "The Surprise of Neruda." *The Sixties,* 7 (Winter, 1964), 18–19.

Briones, A. Valbuena, "La aventura poética de Pablo Neruda." *Cuadernos americanos,* 20 (marzo–abril, 1961), 205–23.

Castro, Raúl Silva, *Pablo Neruda.* Santiago de Chile: Editorial Universitaria, 1964.

Cogo, Bernadarino, "La sterile esperienza marxista di Pablo Neruda." *Letture,* 17 (febbraio, 1962), 83–98.

Darmangeat, Pierre, "Aller à Neruda." *Europe,* 42 (mars–avril, 1964), 75–84.

De Lellis, Mario Jorge, *Pablo Neruda*. Buenos Aires: "La Man-drágora," 1957.

Díaz Arrieta, Hernan, *Los cuatro grandes de la literatura chilena durante el siglo XX: Augusto d'Halmar, Pedro Prado, Gabri-ela Mistral, Pablo Neruda.* Santiago de Chile: Zig-Zag, 1963.

Edwards, Jorge, "La poésie de Neruda." *Europe*, 42 (mars–avril, 1964), 84–91.

Escudero, Alfonso M., "Fuentes para el conocimiento de Neruda." *Mapocho*, 2 (1964), 249–79.

García-Abrines, Luis, "La forma en la última poesía de Neruda." *Revista hispánica moderna*, 25 (octubre, 1959), 303–11.

Gaucheron, Jacques, "Neruda, charpentier d'amour." *Europe*, 44 (juillet–août, 1966), 207–12.

Gicovate, Bernardo, "El yo poético y su significado." *Asomante*, 21 (julio–septiembre, 1965), 40–47.

Jiménez, Juan Ramón, "Un gran mal poeta." *Cuadernos del Congreso por la libertad de la cultura*, 30 (mayo–junio, 1958), 59.

Larrea, Juan, *Del surrealismo a Macchupicchu.* México: Joaquín Mortiz, 1967.

Lozado, Alfredo, "Estilo y poesía de Pablo Neruda, Examen de la interpretación de Amado Alonso de *Residencia en la tierra.*" *Publications of the Modern Language Association of America*, 79 (December, 1964), 648–63.

———, "*Residencia en la tierra*: Algunas correcciónes." *Revista hispánica moderna*, 30 (abril, 1964), 108–18.

Lundkvist, Artur, "Pablo Neruda." *Bonniers Litterära Magasin*, 31 (juli–augusti, 1962), 426–36.

McGrath, Thomas, "The Poetry of Pablo Neruda." *Mainstream*, 15 (June, 1962), 43–47.

Marcenac, Jean, *Pablo Neruda: une étude par Jean Marcenac, choix de textes, inédits, bibliographie, dessins, portraits, fac-similés.* Paris: P. Seghers, 1963.

Meo Zilio, Juan, "Influencia de Sabat Ercasty en Pablo Neruda." *Revista nacional*, 4 (octubre–diciembre, 1959), 589–625.

Monegal, E. Rodríquez, *El viajero inmóvil.* Buenos Aires: Edi-torial Losada, 1966.

Navas-Ruiz, Ricardo, "Neruda y Guillén: Un caso de relaciones literarias." *Revista iberoamericana*, 31 (julio–diciembre, 1965), 251–62.

Paseyro, Ricardo, "El mito de Neruda." *Cuadernos del Congreso por la libertad de la cultura*, 28 (enero–febrero, 1958), 37–48.

———, "Neruda: Vuelta y fin: Respuesta al Sr. Torres Ríoseco." *Cuadernos del Congreso por la libertad de la cultura*, 30 (mayo–junio, 1958), 53–58.

———, Arturo Torres Ríoseco, y Juan Ramón Jiménez, *Mito y*

verdad de Pablo Neruda. México: Asociación Mexicana por la libertad de la cultura, 1958.

Paz Pasamar, Pilar, "Lo, 'chico' en la poesía de Neruda." *Cuadernos hispano-americanos*, 103 (julio, 1958), 95–99.

Peña, Alfredo Cardona, *Pablo Neruda y otros ensayos*. México: Ediciones de Andrea, 1955.

Polt, John H. R., "Elementos gongorinos en 'El gran océano' de Neruda." *Revista hispánica moderna*, 27 (enero, 1961), 23–31.

Rodríguez Fernandez, Mario, "Imagen de la mujer y el amor en un momento de la poesía de Pablo Neruda." *Anales de la Universidad de Chile*, 120 (1962), 74–79.

Rojas, Manuel, "Apunte sobre el sentimiento de soledad en la poesía de Pablo Neruda." *Cuadernos americanos*, 24 (enero–febrero, 1965), 208–18.

Rokha, Pablo de, *Neruda y yo*. Santiago de Chile: Editorial "Multitud," 1955.

Salama, Roberto, *Para una crítica a Pablo Neruda*. Buenos Aires: Cartago, 1957.

Sánchez, Luis Alberto, "Pablo Neruda." *Cuadernos americanos*, 21 (1962), 235–47.

Silva, Castro Raúl, *Pablo Neruda*. Santiago de Chile: Editorial Universitaria, 1964.

Terracini, Lore, "Il *Sumario* di Pablo Neruda e la poesía della memoria." *Paragone*, 16 (agosto, 1965), 37–56.

Torres Ríoseco, Arturo, "Neruda y sus detractores." *Cuadernos del Congreso por la libertad de la cultura*, 30 (mayo–junio, 1958), 49–52.

Undurraga, Antonio de, "Poesía y aquelarre: Neruda y su técnica." *Revista nacional de cultura*, 22 (enero–febrero, 1960), 51–68.

index

"Against the Weather," 2–3, 16–17, 22

"Alberto Rojas Jiménez Comes Flying," 84–85

Andreas-Salomé, Lou, 5, 62, 69

Anne, St., 34, 36

Anonymous center, as source of art, 3, 66–76, 80

Arena Traicionada, La, 11, 89, 98, 105, 107, 111, 114

"Author's Introduction to *The Wedge*," 39

Autobiography of William Carlos Williams, The, 9, 13, 17, 20, 21, 36, 38

Bach, Johann Sebastian, 53

Bachelard, Gaston, xi

"Basis of Faith in Art, The," 41

Baudelaire, Charles: "the daily madness," 4; as subject of poem, 65; quoted, 101

Beethoven, Ludwig von, 53

"Beggars, The," 90

"Beginning on the Short Story (Notes), A," 8, 37

Bergson, Henri, 2, 46

"Between Walls," 39

"Blue Hydrangeas," 77

"Bowl of Roses, The," 69, 74–77

"Brilliant Sad Sun," 39–41

Camus, Albert, 44, 58

Canto General, 89

"Carl Sandburg's Complete Poems," 90

Cézanne, Paul, 5, 68, 80, 111

"Chicory and Daisies," 19

"Comment," 111

"Concerning Landscape," 6

"Crimson Cyclamen, The," 27–31, 32

"Dead, The," 104–5

"Dead in the Square, The," 90, 91

"Death Alone," 84, 101

Definition-descriptions, 6, 47–48

"Dérive du sage, La," 13

Descent of Winter, The, 39

"Detail," 21

Dewey, John, 16

"Dictators, The," 89–90

Ding-poetry, 1–15

Ding-poets: on ontology, 2; on escaping ideas, 2–3, 110–11; on "no ideas but in things," 2–5, 112; and imagism, 3, 5; on keeping poetry impersonal, 3–6, 9, 101, 110; on painters and sculptors, 4–5; on awakening things, 6, 13–14; and romantics, 6–7; and Wordsworth, 6–7; on subjects for poetry, 9–10; on Christianity, 10, 111; on death, 10–11, 112–13; on expression as knowledge, 12; on a rhetoric of things, 12–13; and symbolism, 14; on reconciliation of the individual and the All, 14, 114; on the impermanence of things, 14–15; discussion of, 100–107, 110–15; on religion, 111; on the invisible man, 111–14; definition of poetry, 114; on the use of spoken language in poetry, 114; on the social importance of poetry, 115. *See also* Pablo Neruda, Francis

Ponge, Rainer Maria Rilke, William Carlos Williams
Dingwerdung, 5
"Disproceedings," 101
"Diver," 83
Duino, Rilke at, 113
Duino Elegies, 10, 16, 107
Duncan, Robert, ix

"Earth is Called John, The," 89, 92
"Eau, De l'," 7
"Eighth elegy, The," 8, 66, 72
Einfühlung, 7–9
Elemental Odes, 6, 92, 94–95, 101, 106, 107
Eliot, T. S., 3, 94
"Entrance into Wood," 95, 99–101
"Entretien avec Breton et Reverdy," 45
"Ercilla," 98
Erfahrung, 9, 66–67, 70, 75, 77, 80–81
Erlebnis, 9, 66–67, 70, 73
"Everything Beckons Us to Perceive It," 66
"Excerpts from a Critical Sketch," 27
"Experience, An," 72

"Flowers by the Sea," 28
"For Count Karl Lanckoroński," 73
"For Leonie Zacharias," 61
Francis of Assisi, St., 111
"From: Elephant," 95–98, 106
"Fugitive, The," 94, 109

"Goldsmith, The," 4
"Good Night," 40

Haiku, 100
Handwerker, 4, 68, 79
"Heights of Macchu Picchu, The," 106–9
Homer, 112
Horace, 53
"House of Odes, The," 94–95
"How to Write," 30
Hugo, Victor, 53
"Hunger in the South," 90

"I Am," 89
I Wanted to Write a Poem: The Autobiography of the Works of a Poet, 18, 19, 26
Imagism: 1, 3, 5, 17, 18, 20, 25, 31, 96; Ezra Pound's doctrine of the image, 3; and *Ding*-poetry, 3, 5; as a technique of writing poetry, 5; and Williams, 17, 18, 20, 25, 31; and Neruda, 96
"Infancy and Poetry," 93
"Introduction to Charles Sheeler — Painting — Drawings, Photography," 40
"Invisible Man, The," 7, 10, 84, 93, 112, 114–15

Julien-l'Hospitalier, Saint, 111

"Lamp in the Earth, The," 89
"Last Words of My English Grandmother, The," 35
Leidstadt, 10–11
"Let the Rail Splitter Awake," 84, 90–91, 92
Letters to Merline, 1912–1922, 61–62, 71
Letters of Rainer Maria Rilke, 1892–1910, 62–63, 68, 73, 76–77
Letters of Rainer Maria Rilke, 1910–1926, 3–4, 7, 9, 10, 62, 63, 64–66, 79, 80–81, 98
Letters to a Young Poet, 112
Levertov, Denise, ix–xi
"Liberators, The," 89
"Light from the Sea, A," 99
"Lower Case Cummings," 12

Macchu Picchu, 108, 113
Malherbe, François de, 53
Mallarmé, Stéphane, 13, 53
Marcel, Gabriel, 113
Merton, Thomas, ix
"Mind Hesitant, The," 36–38
Monde muet, le, 43, 114
Moore, Marianne, 6
Mot juste, le, 7, 8, 9, 13–14, 44–45
"Mountain, The," 8
"My Creative Method," 6, 12

"Nantucket," 40
"Natare piscem doces," 46, 51–52
Nausea, 11–12, 85–86
Neruda, Pablo: 83–109; on ontology, 2; on keeping poetry impersonal, 3, 5, 90, 100, 103–4; on subjects for poetry, 9–10; *la arena traicionada*, 11, 89, 98, 105, 107, 111, 114; on using the common idiom in poetry, 12–13, 89, 92, 94, 102–3, 114; and Sartre, 12, 85–86; and Rilke, 12, 88, 95, 98, 100–101, 107; and Stevens, 83, 103; on expressing things, 83–84; on escaping ideas, 83–90, 96, 115; on death, 84–85, 98–99, 104–5, 106–9, 113; on the invisible man, 87, 99–101, 111–12; criticism of "Entrance into Wood," 88–89; on the alienation of men, 88, 106–8; intrusion of self into poetry, 89–91, 101, 107; on the conquered and the conqueror, 89–91, 98, 105–6; effect of Spanish Civil War, 89; and Williams, 90; intrusion of political beliefs into poetry, 90–91, 94, 106; and Whitman, 92; on poetry and being a poet, 93–94, 102, 109; on T. S. Eliot, 94; on Sartre, 94; and imagism, 96; descriptive technique, 96, 103; and Ponge, 100; rejection of early style, 101–2; on symbolism, 101–2; return to simplicity in poetry, 101–3; on religion, 104–5; criticism of "Ode to Bread," 106; on the social importance of poetry, 115
Neruda, Pablo: works discussed, mentioned, and quoted: "A Light from the Sea," 99; "Alberto Rojas Jiménez Comes Flying," 84–85; "The Beggars," 90; *Canto General*, 89; "The Dead," 104–5; "The Dead in the Square," 90, 91; "Death Alone," 84, 101; "The Dictators," 89–90; "Disproceedings," 101; "Diver," 83; "The Earth is Called John,"

89, 92; *Elemental Odes*, 6, 92, 94–95, 101, 106, 107; "Entrance into Wood," 95, 99–101; "Ercilla," 98; "From: Elephant," 95–98, 106; "The Fugitive," 94, 109; "The Heights of Macchu Picchu," 106–9; "The House of Odes," 94–95; "Hunger in the South," 90; "I Am," 89; "Infancy and Poetry," 93; "The Invisible Man," 7, 10, 84, 93, 112, 114–15; "The Lamp in the Earth," 89; "Let the Rail Splitter Awake," 84, 90–91, 92; "The Liberators," 89; "Ode to Bread," 102–6; "Ode to Clarity," 93; "Ode with a Lament," 101; "Our Duty Towards Life," 94; "Poets Celestial," 101–2; *Residence on Earth*, 12, 89, 92, 94, 95, 101; "Reunion Under New Flags," 83; "Ritual of My Legs," 11, 85, 88; "Signifying Shadows," 88–89; "Sonata and Destructions," 101; "Statute of Wine," 2; "Things Breaking," 84; "Three Material Songs," 95; "To Miguel Hernandez," 90; "Toward an Impure Poetry," 1; "Unity," 85; "Viajes al corazon de Quevado y por las costas del mundo," 88; "Walking Around," 86–88
New Poems, 4, 74, 79–80
Nietzsche, Friedrich, 13
"Ninth elegy, The," 1, 14, 80
Notebook of the Pine Grove, The, 6, 46, 100
Notebooks of Malte Laurids Brigge, The, 10, 11–12, 14, 45, 62–66, 67, 68, 70, 88
"Notes for a Sea Shell," 48, 52–54
"Notes from a Talk on Poetry," 18

Objeu, 54–55, 58–59
"Ode to Bread," 102–6
"Ode to Clarity," 93
"Ode with a Lament," 101
Offene, das, 7–8, 11, 65–66, 71, 74, **79, 113**
"Our Duty Towards Life," 94
"Oyster, The," 48–50

"Pages bis," 2
Paris, 62, 68, 80
Parti pris des choses, Le, 7, 45–46
Paterson, 16, 17, 20, 25, 26, 38
Pathetic fallacy, 75–76
"Persian Heliotrope," 77
Platonic poetry, 2–3
"Poets Celestial," 101–2
Ponge, Francis: 43–60; on ontology, 2; on keeping poetry impersonal, 4, 5, 6, 9; ambassador of
the silent world, 5, 13, 43–48, 59,
112, 115; definition-descriptions,
6, 47–48; le mot juste, 7, 8, 9, 13–
14, 44–45; pseudo-civilization,
10; on escaping ideas, 11, 43–44,
45–46, 115; and Valéry, 12; on
use of spoken language in poetry, 12; on expression as
knowledge, 12, 43, 47; on poetic
technique, 12–13, 47–48; definition of poetry, 14, 44, 48, 54; le
monde muet, 43, 114; and the
absurd, 44–45, 58; and Rilke, 45,
100; and Stevens, 47, 55; on ideas
as concrete, 51–52, 56–57; on the
expression of creatures, 51–53;
on art, 52–54; on Bach, 53; on
Beethoven, 53; on Horace, 53;
on Hugo, 53; on language, 53;
on Malherbe, 53; on Mallarmé,
53; on Rameau, 53; on Shelley,
53; objeu, 54–55, 58–59; on
death, 56–60, 112–13; on living
in the present, 59–60; and
Neruda, 100; on the social importance of poetry, 115
Ponge, Francis: works discussed,
mentioned, and quoted: "De
l'eau," 7; "La Dérive du sage,"
13; "Entretien avec Breton et
Reverdy," 45; "My Creative
Method," 6, 12; "Natare piscem
doces," 46, 51–52; The Notebook of the Pine Grove, 6, 46,
100; "Notes for a Sea Shell," 48,
52–54; "The Oyster," 48–50;
"Pages bis," 2; Le Parti pris des
choses, 7, 45–46; "La pratique de
la littérature," 4; La Seine, 44,

45, 48, 53; "The Shrimp in All
Its States," 5; "Snails," 48, 50–52;
"The Sun of the Abyss," 5, 43,
46, 54–60; "Tentative orale," 3,
6, 9
"Pot of Flowers, The," 28
Pound, Ezra: 3, 5, 12, 13, 18, 90;
and doctrine of the image, 3; on
poetic technique, 5; on the pyra-
mid of being, 12; and Williams,
18, 90
"Primavera Trasportata Al Mo-
rale, Della," 41
Pseudo-civilization, 10
"Pratique de la littérature, La," 4
"Prologue to Kora in Hell," 19,
110, 113
Proust, Marcel, 75

Quasha, George, x

Rameau, Jean Philippe, 53
Ransom, John Crowe, 2
Rasles, Père Sebastian, 111
"Red Wheelbarrow, The," 18, 40
Residence on Earth, 12, 89, 92, 94,
95, 101
"Reunion Under New Flags," 83
Rilke, Rainer Maria: 61–82; anonymous center, 3–4, 66–76, 80–82;
on keeping poetry impersonal,
3–5, 6, 9, 66–68, 69–74; on Rodin, 4, 68, 73, 80, 111; on sculp-
ture, 4–5; Handwerker, 4, 68, 79;
on Baudelaire, 4, 65; on Cézanne, 5, 68, 80, 111; Dingwerdung, 5; on poetic technique, 5,
66–68, 69–74, 77–81; Einfühlung,
7–9; das Offene, 7–8, 11, 65–66,
71, 74, 79, 113; on the sleep without a sleeper, 9, 75; Erlebnis, 9,
66–67, 70, 73; on God and religion, 10, 62–65, 111; on Christianity, 10, 62–63; on death, 10–11,
62–66, 73–74, 98, 113; Leidstadt,
10–11; on escaping ideas, 11–12;
and Sartre, 11–12; on awakening
things, 13–14; and Ponge, 45,
100; on art, 61–62; on suffering,
61–65, 68, 111; on time, 63–66,

79; on Baudelaire's "A Carcass," 65; *Weltinnenraum,* 66, 74–77, 80, 81–82; on the act of creation, 66–74; on the artist's medium, 68–69; influence of politics on, 91; and Neruda, 91, 95, 98, 100–101, 107; on St. Francis, 111

Rilke, Rainer Maria: works discussed, mentioned, and quoted: "An Experience," 72; "Baudelaire," 65; "Blue Hydrangeas," 77; "The Bowl of Roses," 69, 74–77; "Concerning Landscape," 6; *Duino Elegies,* 10, 16, 107; "The eighth elegy," 8, 66, 72; "Everything Beckons Us to Perceive It," 66; "For Count Karl Lanckoroński," 73; "For Leonie Zacharias," 61; "The Goldsmith," 4; *Letters of Rainer Maria Rilke, 1892–1910,* 62–63, 68, 73, 76–77; *Letters of Rainer Maria Rilke, 1910–1926,* 3–4, 7, 9, 10, 62, 63, 64–66, 79, 80–81, 98; *Letters to Merline, 1912–1922,* 61–62, 71; *Letters to a Young Poet,* 112; "The Mountain," 8; *New Poems,* 4, 74, 79–80; "The ninth elegy," 1, 14, 80; *The Notebooks of Malte Laurids Brigge,* 10, 11–12, 14, 45, 62–66, 67, 68, 70, 88; "Persian Heliotrope," 77; *Rainer Maria Rilke-Lou Andreas-Salomé, Briefwechsel,* 5; "R.M.R.," 75; "The seventh elegy," 64; *Sonnets to Orpheus,* 9, 15, 69, 80–82; "The Spanish Trilogy," 69–74, 76; "The Stranger," 66–67, 70; "The Temptation," 63; "To Lou Andreas-Salomé," 67; "Turning," 69, 77–80; "Worpswede," 11; *The Young Workman's Letter,* 63

"Ritual of My Legs," 11, 85, 88
"R.M.R.," 75
Rodin, Auguste, 4, 68, 73, 80, 111
Romanticism as predecessor to *Ding*-poetry, 6–7
"Rose, The," 28

Sartre, Jean-Paul: 11, 47, 85–86, 94; and Rilke, 11–12; and Neruda, 12, 85–86
"Sea-Trout and Butterfish," 17–18
Seine, La, 44, 45, 48, 53
Seine, the, 45, 47
Selected Letters of William Carlos Williams, The, 25, 34
"Seventh elegy, The," 64
Shakespeare, William, 111
"Shakespeare," 4
Shelley, Percy, 53
"Shoot it Jimmy!," 21–22
"Shrimp in All Its States, The," 5
"Signifying Shadows," 88–89
"Simplicity of Disorder, The," 4
"Snails," 48, 50–52
"Sonata and Destructions," 101
Sonnets to Orpheus, 9, 15, 69, 80–82
"Spanish Trilogy, The," 69–74, 76
"Statute of Wine," 2
Stevens, Wallace: 5, 47, 55, 83, 103, 105, 110; and Ponge, 47, 55; and Neruda, 83, 105
"Stranger, The," 66–67, 70
"Sun of the Abyss, The," 5, 43, 46, 54–60
Symbolism, 1, 14, 23, 101–2; and *Ding*-poetry, 14; and Williams, 23; and Neruda, 101–2

Tempers, The, 26
"Temptation, The," 63
"Tentative orale," 3, 6, 9
"Things Breaking," 84
"Three Material Songs," 95
"To Lou Andreas-Salomé," 67
"To Miguel Hernandez," 90
"To an Old Jaundiced Woman," 23
"Toward an Impure Poetry," 1
"Tribute to Neruda, the poet collector of seashells," xvii
"Turning," 69, 77–80
"Two Pendants: for the Ears, II; Elena," 31–36

"Unity," 85

182   testimony of the invisible man

Valéry, Paul: 3, 4, 5, 12; definition of poetry, 3, 4; on poetic technique, 5, 12; and Ponge, 12
Variable foot, 26–27
"Viajes al corazon de Quevado y por las costas del mundo," 88

"Walking Around," 86–88
Weltinnenraum, 66, 74–77, 80, 81–82
Whitman, Walt, 92; and Neruda, 92
"Widow's Lament in Springtime, The," 24–25
Williams, William Carlos: 16–42; on escaping ideas, 2–3, 110, 111; on the universal in the local, 2, 16–17, 20, 21, 27, 31, 37–38, 41–42, 111; on keeping poetry impersonal, 3–5, 9, 19, 40; on painting, 4–5, 18; on subjects for poetry, 9; on use of the spoken language in poetry, 12–23, 20–27, 41, 114; moves from imagist position, 17; on the image, 17, 18; and imagism, 17, 18, 20, 25, 31; and Pound, 18, 90; early poems, 17–31, 39–41; definition of poetry, 22, 27; and symbolism, 23; on poetic form, 22, 25–27; on free verse, 25–26; on variable foot, 26–27; flower poems, 27–31; later poems, 31–38, 41–42; on death, 32–36, 112–13; on Christianity, 34; on living in the present, 38–42; and Neruda, 90; on Shakespeare, 111; on Homer, 111–12
Williams, William Carlos: works discussed, mentioned, and quoted: "A Beginning on the Short Story (Notes)," 8, 37; "Against the Weather," 2–3, 16–17, 22; "Author's Introduction to The Wedge," 39; The Autobiography of William Carlos Williams, 9, 13, 17, 20, 21, 36, 38; "Between Walls," 39; "The Basis of Faith in Art," 41; "Bril-

liant Sad Sun," 39–41; "Carl Sandburg's Complete Poems," 90; "Chicory and Daisies," 19; "Comment," 111; "The Crimson Cyclamen," 27–31, 32; "Della Primavera Trasportata Al Morale," 41; The Descent of Winter, 39; "Detail," 21; "Excerpts from a Critical Sketch," 27; "Flowers by the Sea," 28; "Good Night," 40; "How to Write," 30; I Wanted to Write a Poem: The Autobiography of the Works of a Poet, 18, 19, 26; "Introduction to Charles Sheeler — Paintings — Drawings, Photography," 40; "The Last Words of My English Grandmother," 35; "Lower Case Cummings," 12; "The Mind Hesitant," 36–38; "Nantucket," 40; "Notes from a Talk on Poetry," 18; Paterson, 16, 17, 20, 25, 26, 38; "Père Sebastian Rasles," 111; "The Pot of Flowers," 28; "Prologue to Kora in Hell," 19, 110, 113; "The Red Wheelbarrow," 18, 40; "The Rose," 28; "Sea-Trout and Butterfish," 17–18; The Selected Letters of William Carlos Williams, 25, 34; "Shakespeare," 4; "Shoot it Jimmy!," 21–22; "The Simplicity of Disorder," 4; The Tempers, 26; "To an Old Jaundiced Woman," 23; "Tribute to Neruda, the poet collector of seashells," xvii; "Two Pendants: for the Ears, II; Elena," 31–36; "The Widow's Lament in Springtime," 24–25; "The Work of Gertrude Stein," 5
Woolf, Virginia, 1
Wordsworth, William, 6–7, 67; and Ding-poets, 6–7; and Rilke, 67
"Work of Gertrude Stein, The," 5
"Worpswede," 11

Young Workman's Letter, The, 63

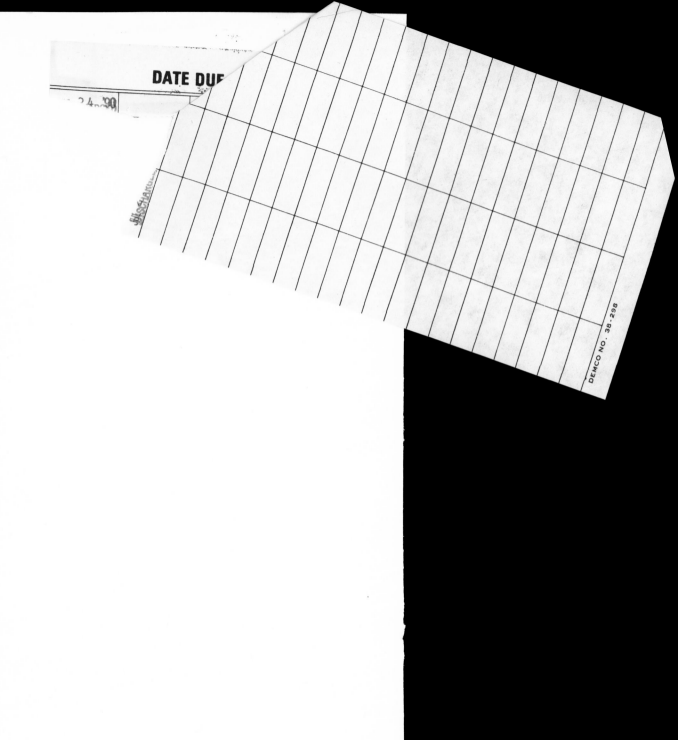